The HIGH-CALCIUM LOW-CALORIE Cookbook

BETTY MARKS

CONTEMPORARY
BOOKS, INC.
CHICAGO • NEW YORK

Library of Congress Cataloging-in-Publication Data

Marks, Betty.
The high-calcium, low-calorie cookbook.

1. High-calcium diet—Recipes. 2. Low-calorie diet—Recipes. I. Title.
RM237.56.M37 1987 641.5′632 87-6670
ISBN 0-8092-4826-3

Betty Marks is coauthor of *The International Menu Diabetic Cookbook.*

Published by Contemporary Books, Inc.
180 North Michigan Avenue, Chicago, Illinois 60601
Manufactured in the United States of America
Library of Congress Catalog Card Number: 87-6670
International Standard Book Number: 0-8092-4826-3

Published simultaneously in Canada by Beaverbooks, Ltd.
195 Allstate Parkway, Valleywood Business Park
Markham, Ontario L3R 4T8 Canada

To my family—the sunshine of my life

CONTENTS

FOREWORD

Osteoporosis has become a household word, but public understanding of this common and devastating disease has been slow. For decades, medical scientists have known ways in which to prevent osteoporosis. But scientific knowledge does little without practical application, and people won't change if they don't understand, if they fear consequences of the changes, or if the change is too unpalatable. Betty Marks, in this splendid book, attacks the ignorance, the fear of side effects, and, most spectacularly, the unpalatability surrounding efforts to induce people to take an adequate amount of calcium in their diets.

While the word osteoporosis has become more familiar, misconceptions still abound. Osteoporosis means inadequate bone mass, which renders the afflicted person vulnerable to broken bones from trivial injury. Half of the women over 45 are so affected. Each year, at least one million Americans break a bone because of osteoporosis, with a resultant economic cost of about six billion dollars.

Public familiarity with the complications of osteoporosis has improved because of advertising campaigns by calcium supplement manufacturers and the dairy industry. The ads have done the public a favor, but also may have contributed to some misunderstandings. Osteoporosis is not a calcium deficiency to be cured by taking large doses of calcium later in life. Osteoporosis is a complex disease with a combination of genetic and environmental influences, such as exercise, hormone balance, other medical problems, and diet.

In part, osteoporosis is a manifestation of poor health and dietary practices over a lifetime. A healthy diet, one that is not only rich in calcium but also adequate in other ways, is essential to bone health. It is essential during childhood, adolescence, and young adulthood when bones grow; it is essential through middle age when bones may be losing strength silently; and it is essential later in life when bones may break from minor injuries.

Every day your body excretes calcium through urine, stool, and perspiration. You cannot absorb all the calcium you take in. Old recommendations to ingest 800 mg per day are too low to cover losses and failure to absorb. But most American diets don't even contain that much. Everybody should get at least 1000 mg and post-menopausal women with susceptibility to osteoporosis should get 1500 mg, nursing mothers even more. When you lose more than you take in, your bones suffer.

Why have Americans damaged their bones by calcium deficient diets? One reason is they didn't know any better—that is no longer a valid reason. Another reason is that they thought a high-calcium diet meant a diet also high in cholesterol, fat, and calories. This cookbook invalidates that reason. Another reason is that they thought any diet that was medically prescribed to be good for you meant tasteless and boring. This cookbook certainly refutes that.

One answer to calcium deficient diets is to take pills, which is certainly better than no answer. Most calcium pills are calcium carbonate—oyster shell calcium. But some people don't absorb calcium carbonate well. Some people are constipated by it. Many people don't like to swallow pills, forget them more often than not, or have other reasons to avoid calcium supplements. For those people and for all who want to manage their health by simple, natural means, pills are not necessary. If there is adequate calcium in your diet, you don't have to take supplements.

Many people reluctantly take pills because they think adequate dietary calcium means four big glasses of milk per day—too much fat, too much cholesterol, too many calories, and boring. Well, pills are boring too, but, as Betty Marks teaches us, pills aren't the only alternative. As you will read in this fun book, you can have a meal of Parmesan Sardine Appetizer, Oriental Snow Pea Soup, Coquilles St. Jacques with Green Beans Amandine, Middle East Cucumber Salad, a Parmesan Popover, and a glass of Mountain Valley (total calories 650), or you can swallow two 500 mg oyster shell pills. Both contain the same amount of calcium. Which sounds best to you?

David F. Fardon, M.D.
Knoxville Orthopedic Clinic
Author, *Osteoporosis, Your Head Start on the Prevention and Treatment of Brittle Bones*

PREFACE

Mother was right to insist you drink your milk! The current calcium craze backs her up, with milk cited as the best source of this vital mineral. Because of the high incidence of osteoporosis, women are particularly concerned with eating the proper foods to ward off this frightening brittle bone disease. At the same time, care must be taken to control high fat and caloric intake contained in many milk products.

The National Institutes of Health have concluded that calcium and the female hormone estrogen are the mainstays of prevention and management of osteoporosis, which afflicts 20 million Americans, most of whom are over 45 years of age. A leading cause of bone fractures, osteoporosis can lead to other complications, causing permanent crippling and death.

Calcium does not regenerate itself, and so adequate quantities must be taken daily. In addition to contributing to strong bones, teeth and muscles, calcium also fights high blood pressure, stress, colon cancer, and a host of other maladies. It is a natural tranquilizer and promotes blood clotting.

A well-balanced diet using low-fat milk products combined with daily sunshine and exercise, and perhaps a one-a-day supplement, will help maintain strong bones and overall good health. The earlier in life such a program is started, the better off one is for maintaining continued good health.

Skim milk or nonfat dry milk, buttermilk, part-skim ricotta and low-fat cottage cheese, plain low-fat or nonfat yogurt, help solve the dilemma of high fat. Delicious dishes can be made with the right combinations of these foods, as the following recipes show. Acidophilus milk, kefir, goat's milk, and soy milk are also low in fat and are good for people with lactose intolerance. Seaweeds, leafy green vegetables, soy nuts, almonds, citrus fruits, sardines and salmon with their bones, oysters, tofu, and whole grains provide additional sources of good nourishment. Vitamins A, B complex, C, and D and the minerals iron, manganese, phosphorous, and potassium are also essential. All these nutrients are best taken from food rather than supplements, many of which have been proven harmful. The dishes in this cookbook are rich in minerals and vitamins.

I am a woman past menopause and I also have diabetes. Therefore, I am a prime candidate for osteoporosis. The meal plan I follow includes plenty of low-fat milk exchanges and other high-calcium foods. My earlier book, *The International Menu Diabetic Cookbook,* contains many recipes that include calcium, and from studying the nutritional needs of diabetics and brittle bone disease victims, I have learned that everything is indeed connected. One hormone is dependent upon another, just as the bones and connective tissues are interdependent, as are the vitamins and minerals we eat. What nourishes one helps nourish the other.

Drink your milk and eat your broccoli! Enjoy many marvelous meals from these recipes, and stay strong and healthy forever!

Betty Marks
New York City
December 1986

ACKNOWLEDGMENTS

Without the help of Linda Fisher-Luther I could not have delivered this book. Her imaginative and nutritious approach to cooking is reflected in the many recipes she contributed. I am grateful for her delicious dishes.

I am indebted to Dr. David Fardon for his foreword and to Hope Warshaw, R.D., whose nutritional evaluation is critical to this book.

I am grateful to my friends who tasted and helped prepare many of the foods included in this volume.

Special thanks go to Dan Bial for the idea.

The United Dairy Industry Association deserves my thanks, too, as does the Dairy Nutrition Council.

The nutritional data used in the book's calculations are based in large part on the DietWise computer program.

INTRODUCTION

Over the last several years we have all been bombarded with reports of deficient calcium consumption. We have also been well informed of the relationship between deficient calcium intake and the increase in bone fractures, especially in older women. Now the challenge is knowing how to increase calcium intake during the younger years to avoid the complications of insufficient calcium intake later in life. One may say that an easy cure-all is simply to take a calcium supplement. As a nutritionist, I encourage individuals who are able to do so to obtain their calcium by making wise food choices. This is easier said than done. Statistically, women are most guilty of insufficient calcium intake. Many studies on calcium consumption show intakes which are often only half of the recommended dietary allowance (RDA). There are several researchers who believe that the RDA for calcium should be increased beyond 800 mg per day for adults.

Why has the consumption of calcium-rich foods decreased? High-calcium foods are often omitted because they are thought to be either unexciting, high in calories, or sometimes just plain inaccessible in our fast-paced world. Beyond good old skim or low-fat milk, the foods thought of as rich in calcium are usually ice cream, cheeses, cream sauces, puddings, etc. Not only are they all high in calcium, but they are also high in fat, calories, and cholesterol. The challenge that Betty Marks had in writing this cookbook was to find fun and creative ways in which to use the often overlooked low-calorie, high-calcium foods. Betty has met this challenge in several ways. Her recipes provide maximum calcium by incorporating low-fat, low-cholesterol alternatives, such as skim and evaporated skim milk, nonfat dry milk, low-fat cottage cheese and yogurt, as well as other commonly available foods. Betty has also incorporated many of the lesser known high-calcium foods into tasty appetizers, entrees, desserts, and more. These include tofu, figs, dandelion greens, sardines, and salmon. Finally, Betty introduces us to new and unusual products, which increase the variety of foods from which we can choose.

The facts conclude that more calcium is needed in our daily diet. With this high-calcium, low-fat cookbook in hand, the opportunity is yours to make the task of consuming sufficient calcium enjoyable, while at the same time building and maintaining strong bones and achieving optimal health.

Hope S. Warshaw, M.M.Sc., R.D.
Nutrition Consultant
Boston, Massachusetts

1
APPETIZERS

Any of these appetizers may be used as the first course of a meal or as an hors d'oeuvre or snack. Consult the nutrient information at the end of each recipe to determine which choices will fit in with your meals for the day. Try a dollop of Avocado Smoothie on a baked potato or serve Black Bean and Salmon Dip appetizer on a bed of lettuce for a luncheon main dish. Dare to be different and make your own delicious food combinations.

The dips may be served with raw vegetables such as string beans, carrot sticks, zucchini sticks, red or green bell pepper strips, radishes, cauliflower or broccoli florets, or with low-fat whole wheat crackers, wasa bread, pita, tortillas, or toast. Celery, bok choy, and fennel are good for stuffing, too.

The inventive chef will want to try combinations of low-fat cottage cheese, ricotta, or yogurt with different vegetable purees and herbs. Sardines and salmon lend themselves to infinite variations when combined with fresh lemon or lime juice or mixed with high-calcium beans.

Many of the spreads may be thinned with a bit more milk or yogurt to make a succulent sauce or dressing. An extra sprinkle of parsley or grated cheese will add still more calcium.

DIPS AND SPREADS

AVOCADO SMOOTHIE

1 small avocado, peeled and pitted (1 scant cup)
1 tablespoon fresh lemon juice
1 tablespoon nonfat dry milk
1 tablespoon minced scallion
1 cup low-fat cottage cheese
Salt and freshly ground black pepper to taste
3 dashes cayenne pepper

Puree all ingredients in blender or food processor until smooth. Chill and serve with raw vegetables or whole wheat or rice crackers.

Makes 2 cups or 16 2-tablespoon servings

Per serving:	*Calcium* (mg)	*Fat* (g)	*Chol* (mg)	*Carbo* (g)	*Protein* (g)	*Calories*
	26	2	.6	1.5	2	32

BLACK BEAN AND SALMON DIP

8 corn tortillas
1 1-pound can black beans, rinsed and drained
1 7-ounce can pink salmon with bones, drained
2 tablespoons safflower oil
¼ cup fresh lime juice
¼ cup chopped fresh Italian parsley
½ teaspoon onion powder
½ teaspoon celery salt
¾ teaspoon ground cumin
¾ teaspoon minced garlic
½ teaspoon grated lime zest
¼ teaspoon dried red pepper flakes
¼ teaspoon chili pepper

Cut tortillas into triangles and toast in 350°F oven until crisp. Mix together the drained beans and salmon, flaking the salmon with a fork. Mix in the oil and lime juice and all remaining ingredients except the tortillas. Chill to blend flavors. Serve with chips. May also be used as an entree for 4, served on a bed of romaine lettuce.

Makes 2½ cups or 20 2-tablespoon servings

Per serving:	*Calcium* (mg)	*Fat* (g)	*Chol* (mg)	*Carbo* (g)	*Protein* (g)	*Calories*
	36	2.2	2	6.8	3.6	60

CAVIAR CHEESE DIP

¾ cup part-skim ricotta cheese
¼ cup low-fat cottage cheese
1 teaspoon fresh lemon juice
2 ounces red lumpfish caviar

Blend the cheeses with the lemon juice. Place in serving dish and top with caviar, or mix, as desired. Serve with rice crackers or whole wheat crisps or as an appetizer spread on baked potato skins or stuffed in celery. (It is also delicious as a topping for baked potatoes.)

Makes 1 cup or 8 2-tablespoon servings

Per Serving:	*Calcium* (mg)	*Fat* (g)	*Chol* (mg)	*Carbo* (g)	*Protein* (g)	*Calories*
	87	3	7.5	0	5.5	56

CHILI CON QUESO

½ cup orange-flavored Yogurt Sour Cream (see note below)
2 tablespoons chopped, seeded jalapeño pepper
1 clove garlic, minced
2 tablespoons minced onion or scallion

Stir together all ingredients. Serve with crudités or toasted tortilla chips.

Note: To make orange-flavored Yogurt Sour Cream, follow the recipe for Yogurt Sour Cream (see index), using 1 cup plain nonfat yogurt and 2 tablespoons concentrated frozen orange juice.

Makes ¾ cup or 12 1-tablespoon servings

Per serving:	*Calcium* (mg)	*Fat* (g)	*Chol* (mg)	*Carbo* (g)	*Protein* (g)	*Calories*
	36	.3	1.2	2.6	1	17

CLAM CHEESE DIP

½ cup chopped clams
¼ cup low-fat cottage cheese
¾ cup part-skim ricotta cheese
¼ cup chopped onion
1 clove garlic, sliced
½ teaspoon celery salt
1 teaspoon drained capers
1 teaspoon fresh lemon juice
1 teaspoon anchovy paste
¼ teaspoon dried thyme
Dash white pepper
Dash cayenne pepper
Paprika
Sprig parsley

Combine all ingredients except paprika and parsley in blender or food processor. Garnish with dusting of paprika and place parsley sprig in center. Serve with vegetable crudités or crackers.

Makes 1 cup or 8 2-tablespoon servings

Per serving:	*Calcium* (mg)	*Fat* (g)	*Chol* (mg)	*Carbo* (g)	*Protein* (g)	*Calories*
	80	2.2	6.5	2.1	5.6	52

CONFETTI VEGETABLE DIP

1 cup part-skim ricotta cheese
½ cup plain low-fat yogurt
½ cup shredded carrot
¼ cup sliced scallion
2 tablespoons chopped red bell pepper
2 tablespoons chopped green bell pepper
2 tablespoons finely chopped celery
¼ teaspoon salt
⅛ teaspoon freshly ground black pepper

Mix ricotta and yogurt until smooth. Add remaining ingredients. Cover and refrigerate to combine flavors until ready to serve. Serve with additional fresh vegetables, whole wheat crackers, or pita bread triangles.

Makes about 1¾ cups or 14 2-tablespoon servings

Per serving:	Calcium (mg)	Fat (g)	Chol (mg)	Carbo (g)	Protein (g)	Calories
	69	1.5	6	2.5	2.5	34

FANCY FENNEL DIP

1 cup low-fat cottage cheese
½ cup grated sharp cheddar or Colby cheese
2 tablespoons buttermilk
1 tablespoon nonfat dry milk
1 teaspoon fennel or dill seeds
¼ teaspoon dry mustard
⅛ teaspoon freshly ground black pepper
Pinch cayenne pepper
1 tablespoon chopped scallions
Paprika
Minced fresh parsley

Blend all ingredients except paprika and parsley in food processor and chill. Garnish with a little paprika and minced parsley.

Makes 2 cups or 16 2-tablespoon servings

Per serving:	Calcium (mg)	Fat (g)	Chol (mg)	Carbo (g)	Protein (g)	Calories
	40	13	4.5	.8	2.8	27

VEGETABLE GUACAMOLE

½ cup peeled, pitted, and sliced avocado
1 tablespoon fresh lime juice
½ cup fresh peas
½ cup broccoli florets
¼ cup peeled, chopped, and seeded ripe tomatoes
¼ cup chopped fresh coriander leaves (cilantro)
1 clove garlic, minced
1 small green chili, seeded and sliced
2 tablespoons nonfat dry milk
2 tablespoons chopped onion
10 corn tortillas

Using a fork, mash avocado slices with lime juice. Blanch peas and broccoli (any other green vegetable may be used) and puree. Mix with avocados and add remaining ingredients except the tortillas. Cut these into wedges and spread on cookie sheet to bake until crisp in 350°F oven. Serve with guacamole dip.

Makes about 2 cups or 10 3-tablespoon servings

Per serving (includes one tortilla):	Calcium (mg)	Fat (g)	Chol (mg)	Carbo (g)	Protein (g)	Calories
	21	2.9	.1	13.8	3.6	109

HEAVENLY HUMMUS

2 cups cooked garbanzo beans (chick-peas) (if canned, rinse and drain)
2 tablespoons buttermilk
¼ cup toasted sesame seeds
3 tablespoons fresh lemon juice
1 teaspoon sesame oil
1 tablespoon low-sodium soy sauce
2 cloves garlic, sliced
1 teaspoon ground cumin
Pinch freshly ground black pepper
3 dashes cayenne pepper

Mix all ingredients in food processor until well blended. Add more buttermilk to adjust consistency. Serve with raw vegetables, whole wheat crackers, or pita bread.

Makes 1 cup or 8 2-tablespoon servings

Per serving:	*Calcium* (mg)	*Fat* (g)	*Chol* (mg)	*Carbo* (g)	*Protein* (g)	*Calories*
	29	2.6	.3	11.7	5	85

LIPTAUER CHEESE

½ cup part-skim ricotta cheese
2 tablespoons nonfat dry milk
1 tablespoon safflower oil
1 teaspoon drained capers
1 teaspoon Hungarian sweet paprika
½ teaspoon anchovy paste
1 tablespoon caraway seeds
1 tablespoon chopped scallion
Salt and freshly ground pepper to taste

Mix all ingredients together and refrigerate for about 8 hours. Serve with whole wheat or rice crackers or good rye bread.

Makes 1 cup or 8 2-tablespoon servings

Per serving:	Calcium (mg)	Fat (g)	Chol (mg)	Carbo (g)	Protein (g)	Calories
	55	2.6	5	1.5	2.2	40

MISO MANIA

1 cup tofu (bean curd), cut into chunks
3 tablespoons miso (fermented barley or soy paste, see Chapter 12)
¼ cup water
1 teaspoon sesame oil
1 tablespoon fresh lemon juice
¼ teaspoon crushed red pepper flakes
2 scallions, chopped
2 tablespoons crunchy peanut butter
3 tablespoons plain low-fat yogurt
Alfalfa sprouts

Beat all ingredients except alfalfa sprouts in food processor or blender until smooth. Serve on warm pita bread triangles with alfalfa sprout topping or over fresh garden vegetables.

Makes 2 cups or 16 2-tablespoon servings

Per serving:	Calcium (mg)	Fat (g)	Chol (mg)	Carbo (g)	Protein (g)	Calories
	28	1.9	.2	1.2	1.9	23

PARMESAN SARDINE APPETIZER

1 3¾-ounce can water-packed sardines with bones
2 tablespoons plain low-fat yogurt
2 tablespoons grated Parmesan or sapsago cheese
1 tablespoon chopped scallion
1 teaspoon Dijon mustard
1 teaspoon grated lemon zest
3 teaspoons fresh lime or lemon juice
Freshly ground black pepper to taste
Dash cayenne pepper
1 teaspoon toasted sesame seeds
4 romaine lettuce or spinach leaves

Drain sardines and mash with a fork. Stir in yogurt, cheese, and all remaining ingredients except sesame seeds and lettuce. Place in small serving bowl. Top with sprinkling of seeds and chill a few hours. Make individual servings on bed of romaine lettuce or spinach leaves as first course or serve as hors d'oeuvres on Japanese rice crackers.

Makes 4 first-course servings

Per serving:	*Calcium* (mg)	*Fat* (g)	*Chol* (mg)	*Carbo* (g)	*Protein* (g)	*Calories*
	124	3.1	23.7	1.9	5	49

PICKLE PEPPER SPREAD

¼ cup low-fat cottage cheese
¾ cup part-skim ricotta cheese
¼ cup grated sharp cheddar cheese
1 teaspoon Dijon mustard
2 tablespoons chopped dill pickles
2 tablespoons chopped pimiento
2 tablespoons chopped green pepper

Combine all ingredients in food processor, saving some of the pimiento and green pepper for garnish when serving. Chill and serve as spread on rice crackers or toast.

Makes about 1½–2 cups or 12–16 2-tablespoon servings

Per serving:	Calcium (mg)	Fat (g)	Chol (mg)	Carbo (g)	Protein (g)	Calories
	71	2.5	9	1.1	3.3	40

SIMON'S SIMPLE SALMON DIP

1 cup low-fat cottage cheese
5 ounces canned pink salmon with bones
1 tablespoon minced scallion or chives
2 tablespoons plain low-fat yogurt or buttermilk
1 teaspoon fresh lemon juice
2 tablespoons diced dill pickles
Dash Tabasco
Salt and freshly ground pepper to taste
Parsley for garnish

Combine all ingredients except parsley in blender or food processor. Adjust seasoning. Garnish with parsley. Serve with rice crackers, whole wheat crackers or toast, or fresh vegetables.

Makes 2 cups or 16 2-tablespoon servings

Per serving:	Calcium (mg)	Fat (g)	Chol (mg)	Carbo (g)	Protein (g)	Calories
	32	.7	4	.9	3.6	25

SUZANNE'S SPINACH APPETIZER

10 ounces fresh spinach, washed and trimmed
12 ounces firm tofu (bean curd), cut into chunks
3 tablespoons fresh lime or lemon juice
2 tablespoons safflower oil
2 cloves garlic, minced
1 teaspoon dried oregano, crushed
¼ teaspoon salt
Dash freshly grated nutmeg
Freshly ground black pepper to taste
Extra spinach leaves
1 red bell pepper, sliced into julienne strips

Place all ingredients except extra spinach leaves and red pepper strips in a food processor and blend together. Place in refrigerator to combine flavors. When ready to serve, place on bed of spinach leaves and surround with pepper strips or place strips in a small cup in center of dip. Nice with other fresh garden vegetables, too.

Makes about 3 cups or 12 ¼-cup servings

Per serving:	*Calcium* (mg)	*Fat* (g)	*Chol* (mg)	*Carbo* (g)	*Protein* (g)	*Calories*
	88	3.7	0	3.3	3.8	56

TOMATO DIP

½ cup plain low-fat yogurt
¾ cup low-fat cottage cheese, rinsed and drained
¼ cup tomato or V-8 juice
1 tablespoon dried onion flakes
¼ teaspoon dry mustard
1 teaspoon fresh lime juice
2 tablespoons tomato paste
1 teaspoon chopped dill pickles
1 teaspoon low-sodium soy sauce
1 teaspoon chopped fresh parsley

Fold the yogurt into the drained cottage cheese and then blend in remaining ingredients, sprinkling the parsley on top as garnish. Serve with crudités, whole wheat crackers, or bread, or use as sauce for cooked fish or vegetables.

Makes 2 cups or 16 2-tablespoon servings

Per serving:	*Calcium* (mg)	*Fat* (g)	*Chol* (mg)	*Carbo* (g)	*Protein* (g)	*Calories*
	20	.6	1	1.5	1.8	19

TRICOLOR YOGURT LOAF

4 cups plain Yogurt Sour Cream (see note below)
1 envelope unflavored gelatin
¼ cup cold water
1 tablespoon crystalline fructose
½ cup Crème Fraîche (see index)
1 teaspoon salt
3 tablespoons walnut oil
Dash white pepper
⅓ cup sliced scallions, including green
2 tablespoons minced fresh parsley
⅓ cup peeled, seeded, and chopped tomatoes
About 1 cup romaine lettuce or spinach greens
3 tablespoons chopped toasted almonds

When yogurt has drained, transfer to a large mixing bowl. In a cup, soften gelatin in cold water. In a small saucepan, mix the gelatin, fructose, Crème Fraîche, and salt. Stir over gentle heat until gelatin dissolves. Turn into the yogurt along with walnut oil and pepper. Stir to blend. In the meantime, line a 5-inch by 8-inch loaf pan with plastic wrap, extending it over the sides of the pan. Then pour one-third of the yogurt mixture into the loaf pan. Combine scallions with parsley and sprinkle one-third of the mixture over the yogurt in pan. Cover with half of remaining yogurt. Spread over this half of the chopped tomatoes. Over this layer spread rest of the yogurt. Fold the plastic wrap over the top and refrigerate for about 4 hours.

When ready to serve, or a few hours ahead of time, invert loaf pan onto lettuce-lined serving plate. Garnish the top of the yogurt loaf with three alternating bands of scallions with parsley, tomatoes, and almonds. Serve with crisp crackers as an appetizer or a luncheon dish. Will keep well refrigerated up to 2 days.

Note: To make 4 cups plain Yogurt Sour Cream, follow the recipe for Yogurt Sour Cream (see index), using 8 cups plain low-fat yogurt.

Serves 8

Per serving:	*Calcium* (mg)	*Fat* (g)	*Chol* (mg)	*Carbo* (g)	*Protein* (g)	*Calories*
	274	9.9	12	12	8.9	170

HORS D'OEUVRES

CORNY TOFU STICKS

Vegetable spray
1 pound firm tofu (bean curd)
1 cup nonfat dry milk
2 eggs (1 yolk only)
2 tablespoons vegetable oil
1 tablespoon crystalline fructose
½ cup buttermilk
¼ cup whole wheat flour
1½ teaspoons baking powder
1½ cups cornmeal

Preheat oven to 425°F. Coat 2 cornstick pans (6 sticks each) or one 8-inch square pan with vegetable spray. In a blender or food processor, mix the tofu, nonfat dry milk, eggs, oil, fructose, and buttermilk. Process until smooth. Mix the dry ingredients together, then combine with tofu mixture. Stir to mix gently. Bake the sticks for 20 minutes or the square pan for 25–30 minutes, until the top is brown and springs back when touched lightly.

Makes 12 sticks or 16 2-inch squares

Per serving:	*Calcium* (mg)	*Fat* (g)	*Chol* (mg)	*Carbo* (g)	*Protein* (g)	*Calories*
	102	4.8	24	18.6	6.7	142

OYSTERS ON THE HALF SHELL

1 dozen fresh bluepoint or other oysters
Lemon wedges
Grated horseradish

Purchase oysters from a reliable fish market, making certain they are alive and fresh. Keep refrigerated until ready to serve, shuck (see Chapter 12), and serve on the half shell on a bed of ice with lemon wedges, horseradish, or any other sauce desired.

Makes 2 6-oyster servings

Per serving (6 oysters):	*Calcium* (mg)	*Fat* (g)	*Chol* (mg)	*Carbo* (g)	*Protein* (g)	*Calories*
	84	1.8	48	3	7.8	60

SARDINE SQUASH

4 cups raw acorn or butternut squash (cooks down to 2 cups)
1 tablespoon vegetable oil
½ cup chopped onion
1 clove garlic, minced
¼ cup Chicken Stock (see index)
4 tablespoons fresh lime or lemon juice
2 teaspoons grated lemon zest
1 teaspoon dried dill weed
Salt and freshly ground pepper to taste
1 7½-ounce can sardines with bones in tomato sauce
Lemon slices
Parsley sprigs
4 romaine lettuce or spinach leaves (optional)

Peel and seed the squash and grate to make 4 cups. Heat the oil in a large nonstick skillet with onion and garlic. Add squash, broth, lime or lemon juice, zest, and dill. Cover and steam for 3 minutes. Add salt and pepper, then remove from heat and turn out onto plates. Arrange the sardines and tomato sauce over the squash and garnish with lemon slices and parsley sprigs. Place on lettuce or spinach leaves, if desired.

Serves 4 as an appetizer

Per serving:	Calcium (mg)	Fat (g)	Chol (mg)	Carbo (g)	Protein (g)	Calories
	166	7.1	43	13.7	9	147

SARDINE-STUFFED MUSHROOMS

12 medium-sized mushroom caps (stems removed), wiped clean
1 3¾-ounce can water-packed sardines including bones, drained
¼ teaspoon dried dill weed
2 teaspoons Dijon mustard
1 tablespoon fresh lime juice
12 capers, drained and chopped
Parsley sprigs or fresh chopped parsley
Paprika

Mash sardines with the dill, mustard, lime juice, and capers. Stuff into the mushroom caps. Garnish with parsley and a dash of paprika.

Makes 12 servings

Per serving:	Calcium (mg)	Fat (g)	Chol (mg)	Carbo (g)	Protein (g)	Calories
	23	.6	7	.6	1.6	14

STUFFED GRAPE LEAVES

2 tablespoons vegetable oil, divided
¾ cup minced onion
⅓ cup brown rice
1¼ cups water
1 tablespoon sunflower seeds
1 tablespoon minced fresh parsley
1 tablespoon chopped fresh mint *or* 1 teaspoon dried
Freshly ground pepper to taste
1 tablespoon raisins
15 grape leaves
2 tablespoons cold water
Lemon wedges

In a nonstick skillet, heat 1 tablespoon of vegetable oil and sauté onion in it. Add uncooked rice and stir until grains are coated. Add 1¼ cups water and bring to simmer. Cover pan and cook until rice is tender and all water absorbed, about 20 to 30 minutes. Add more water if necessary. Lightly brown sunflower seeds in another skillet and add to cooked rice with parsley, mint, pepper, and raisins.

In the meantime, blanch grape leaves in boiling water and separate. Place on paper toweling dull side up. Stuff each leaf with rice mixture to form small bundles. Fold so that each leaf is wrapped around rice. Stack stuffed leaves seam side down in a large casserole. Add 2 tablespoons cold water and sprinkle with remaining tablespoon of oil. Cover and simmer 30 minutes. Serve at room temperature with lemon wedges.

Makes 15 servings

Per serving:	*Calcium* (mg)	*Fat* (g)	*Chol* (mg)	*Carbo* (g)	*Protein* (g)	*Calories*
	30	2.2	0	5.5	1.2	44

2
SOUPS

Soup may begin a meal or may be the main course, served with a bright green salad and a good hearty bread, muffins, or crisp crackers. Soup may be thin, such as Oriental Snow Pea Soup, or thick, such as Mexican Corn Chowder and Connie's Iowa Bean Soup. The creamy Salmon Bisque is rich and delicious and provides a big calcium kick.

For the cream soups, buttermilk, yogurt, and skim milk are all interchangeable, according to your taste. Remember, yogurt should not be boiled! When making soups that call for it, just heat quickly at the end of the preparation and serve warm. Add nonfat dry milk to any soup for still more calcium.

Vegetables other than those specified may be substituted—celery or mushrooms instead of carrots, broccoli in place of zucchini, fish instead of shrimp, lobster rather than fish. Most will work well with a simple adjustment of spices and seasonings.

Colorful garnishes on top of the soup can give extra calcium and appeal—try a teaspoon of chopped parsley or basil, or red and green bell peppers chopped fine, or some thinly shredded carrots, or a sprinkling of paprika or nutmeg.

In a pinch, if you're caught short of a specified stock, use Vogue Instant Chicken or Vegetable Flavored Base, available in most health food stores and supermarkets.

Note: The blender or food processor is indispensable in making pureed soups, but never pour hot liquid directly into it. Let the soup cool, then add a little at a time and return to saucepan when mixed.

ASPARAGUS POTAGE

½ cup cooked potato, cut into chunks
½ cup chopped onion
2 cups Vegetable Stock or Chicken Stock (see index)
2 cups fresh asparagus, trimmed and cut into 2-inch pieces
¼ cup chopped carrot
2 tablespoons whole wheat flour
Freshly ground black pepper
2 tablespoons dry sherry or vermouth
½ teaspoon salt
Dash cayenne pepper
½ teaspoon grated lemon zest
Dash dried thyme
Dash dried mint
2 cups buttermilk
Fresh chopped parsley or chives

Cook potato and onion in the stock for about 10 minutes. Add remaining ingredients except buttermilk and parsley or chives. Bring to boil and cook until asparagus is tender, about 5 minutes. Remove from heat, let cool, and a little at a time puree in blender or food processor, then return to saucepan and stir in buttermilk. Garnish with chopped parsley or chives. Serve warm or chilled.

Makes about 4½ cups or 4 1⅛-cup servings

Per serving:	*Calcium* (mg)	*Fat* (g)	*Chol* (mg)	*Carbo* (g)	*Protein* (g)	*Calories*
	172	2.7	8	16.6	7.2	116

BUTTERMILK BROCCOLI SOUP

1 teaspoon vegetable oil
½ cup chopped onion
1 clove garlic, minced
3 cups cut-up broccoli florets and stems
2 cups buttermilk
1 teaspoon cumin seed
Pinch freshly grated nutmeg
1 tablespoon chopped fresh parsley
1 tablespoon diced red bell pepper

In nonstick skillet, heat the oil and sauté onion and garlic in it. Add broccoli to pan and toss for 1 minute. Turn into food processor with remaining ingredients except parsley and peppers and blend until smooth. Serve with garnish of parsley and peppers.

Makes about 6 cups or 4 1½-cup servings

Per serving:	*Calcium* (mg)	*Fat* (g)	*Chol* (mg)	*Carbo* (g)	*Protein* (g)	*Calories*
	242	3	5	18.4	11.2	129

CARIOCA BEAN SOUP

2 cups dried black beans
3 cups Vegetable Stock or Beef Stock (see index)
1 large onion, chopped
2 stalks celery, chopped
1 bay leaf
7 cups water
¼ teaspoon salt
Dash freshly ground black pepper
1 teaspoon chopped jalapeño pepper ***or***
½ teaspoon crushed dried red pepper
2 tablespoons dry sherry
10 slices lemon
Chopped parsley

Cover beans with salted water by two inches and let soak overnight, draining periodically and replacing water. When ready to prepare soup, drain again. Place the drained beans in a large kettle with all the ingredients but sherry, lemon, and parsley. Cover and bring to boil. Skim off any froth that accumulates, and simmer covered over low heat for about 3 hours or until beans and vegetables are tender. Remove from pot, let cool, and little by little puree in blender or food processor. Adjust seasoning, add sherry, and return to kettle to warm. Serve topped with lemon slice and sprinkling of parsley.

Makes 10 cups or 10 1-cup servings

Per serving:	*Calcium* (mg)	*Fat* (g)	*Chol* (mg)	*Carbo* (g)	*Protein* (g)	*Calories*
	26	.4	0	10.1	3.5	59

CHILLY CANNELLINI SOUP

1 15-ounce can cannellini beans (white kidney beans), drained and rinsed
½ cup plain low-fat yogurt
¾ cup skim milk
1 clove garlic, chopped
1 small onion, chopped
1 tablespoon finely chopped fresh basil *or* 1 teaspoon dried
Salt and freshly ground black pepper to taste
Dash cayenne pepper
Extra yogurt
1 tablespoon chopped fresh parsley

Place all ingredients except extra yogurt and parsley in food processor or blender and puree until smooth. Pour into a bowl and chill 2–3 hours before serving. Serve with dollop of yogurt and sprinkling of parsley.

Makes about 2 cups or 4 ½-cup servings

Per serving:	*Calcium* (mg)	*Fat* (g)	*Chol* (mg)	*Carbo* (g)	*Protein* (g)	*Calories*
	148	1	3	24.5	9.8	143

COTTAGE CHEESE SOUP

1 tablespoon Best Butter (see index)
1 small onion, chopped fine
1 stalk celery, chopped
1 green bell pepper, cored, seeded, and chopped fine
½ teaspoon salt
¼ teaspoon freshly ground black pepper
¼ teaspoon Hungarian sweet paprika
1 cup water
2 cups skim milk
½ cup low-fat cottage cheese
2 tablespoons part-skim ricotta cheese

Heat the Best Butter in a nonstick skillet and cook the onion, celery, and green peppers in it for 5 minutes or until tender. Add the salt, pepper, paprika, water, and milk. Cover and cook over low heat about 15 minutes. Just before serving, add the cottage cheese and ricotta, stirring to blend. Do not let boil.

Makes 4 cups or 4 1-cup servings

Per serving:	*Calcium* (mg)	*Fat* (g)	*Chol* (mg)	*Carbo* (g)	*Protein* (g)	*Calories*
	202	4.3	9.3	11.1	9.4	119

CREAM OF MUSHROOM SOUP

1 teaspoon Best Butter (see index)
¼ cup minced onion
2 cups thinly sliced fresh mushrooms
⅓ cup chopped celery
2 cups skim milk
2 tablespoons nonfat dry milk
1½ tablespoons whole wheat flour or cream of wheat
½ teaspoon salt
Dash freshly ground black pepper
Dash cayenne pepper
Dash freshly grated nutmeg
2 tablespoons dry sherry
Paprika
1 tablespoon chopped fresh parsley

Heat Best Butter in a nonstick saucepan and in it sauté onions and celery and then add mushroom slices, cooking until tender. Mix remaining ingredients except paprika and parsley in blender or food processor and then add the mushroom mixture and blend again. Pour into the saucepan and heat gently until soup thickens, stirring. Garnish with paprika and parsley to serve.

Makes 4 cups or 4 1-cup servings

Per serving:	*Calcium* (mg)	*Fat* (g)	*Chol* (mg)	*Carbo* (g)	*Protein* (g)	*Calories*
	192	1.5	4	14.2	7	96

CREAMY CARROT SOUP

2 teaspoons Best Butter (see index)
1 teaspoon whole wheat flour
2 cups scraped and sliced carrots
2 cups Vegetable Stock (see index)
Pinch salt
1 sprig fresh thyme *or* ¼ teaspoon dried, crumbled
1 bay leaf
½ teaspoon fresh ginger (optional)
1 teaspoon concentrated frozen orange juice
Freshly ground pepper
1 cup skim milk
2 tablespoons nonfat dry milk
Few sprigs fresh mint *or* ½ teaspoon dried mint or fresh chopped parsley

In nonstick saucepan, heat Best Butter and stir in whole wheat flour. Add carrots, Vegetable Stock, and the salt and bring to boil. Add thyme, bay leaf, and ginger, if desired. Reduce heat and simmer until tender, about 8 minutes. With slotted spoon, remove ¼ cup of carrots and reserve for garnish. Skim off any froth that accumulates. Let cool, remove bay leaf, and pour into food processor a little at a time, to blend. Return to saucepan, add orange juice concentrate, pepper to taste, and the milk. Heat through, stirring. Serve with garnish of fresh mint or parsley and reserved carrots. May also be served cold.

Makes 4 cups or 4 1-cup servings

Per serving:	*Calcium* (mg)	*Fat* (g)	*Chol* (mg)	*Carbo* (g)	*Protein* (g)	*Calories*
	151	3.5	6	20	3.6	108

CUCUMBER BUTTERMILK SOUP

2 cups peeled, seeded, and chopped cucumbers
4 cups buttermilk
1 tablespoon fresh lemon juice
2 tablespoons chopped scallion
1 tablespoon chopped fresh mint *or* 1 teaspoon dried
1 tablespoon chopped fresh dill *or* 1 teaspoon dried
1 teaspoon ground cumin seed
Dash white pepper
1 tablespoon fresh chopped parsley

Place all ingredients except parsley in blender or food processor and blend until smooth. Garnish with fresh parsley. Serve cold.

Makes 5 cups or 4 1¼-cup servings

Per serving:	*Calcium* (mg)	*Fat* (g)	*Chol* (mg)	*Carbo* (g)	*Protein* (g)	*Calories*
	297	2.2	9	13.4	8.3	109

KALE SOUP

½ pound fresh kale, well washed
4 cups Chicken Stock (see index)
Pinch salt
¼ teaspoon freshly ground black pepper
3 medium potatoes, peeled and sliced thin
1 teaspoon safflower oil
2 cloves garlic, minced
6 slices lemon
Dash cayenne pepper

Discard tough stems and any discolored kale leaves. Shred or chop kale very fine. Place all ingredients but lemon and cayenne in a saucepan and cook until potatoes are tender. Remove them and mash, then return to the broth and bring to a boil. Serve with lemon slices and dash of cayenne.

Makes 6 cups or 6 1-cup servings

Per serving:	*Calcium* (mg)	*Fat* (g)	*Chol* (mg)	*Carbo* (g)	*Protein* (g)	*Calories*
	114	2.3	1	19.3	5.7	114

LOBSTER AND TOMATO BISQUE

1 lobster, about 1½-2 pounds
2 cups canned Italian plum tomatoes
¼ cup finely chopped onion
1 bay leaf
2 large fresh leaves basil, chopped, *or* ½ teaspoon dried
2 cups skim milk
2 tablespoons part-skim ricotta cheese
Salt and freshly ground pepper to taste

Cut the lobster into pieces (see Chapter 12) and place in a heavy saucepan with the tomatoes, onion, bay leaf, and basil. Bring to a simmer and cook over low heat for 10 minutes, just until the lobster is cooked (the shells will turn red). Do not overcook. Remove from heat, take out the lobster pieces and discard bay leaf. With a small fork, extract the lobster meat from the shells, cut into small pieces, and reserve, discarding shells. (This is a little messy, but worth it.) Puree the tomato sauce in blender or food processor and pour into a clean saucepan. Add the milk, stir in ricotta, and bring to a simmer. Add the lobster meat, season with salt and pepper, and serve warm.

Makes 6 cups or 4 1½-cup servings

Per serving:	*Calcium* (mg)	*Fat* (g)	*Chol* (mg)	*Carbo* (g)	*Protein* (g)	*Calories*
	201	1.6	40	12.2	13	115

GREEN GODDESS SOUP

3 medium new potatoes (about ¾ pound) *or* 1½ cups, sliced
1 teaspoon vegetable oil
¼ cup minced onion
2 cups chopped watercress
2 cups chopped fresh parsley
1 cup Chicken Stock or Vegetable Stock (see index)
¼ teaspoon ground cumin seed
Few dashes cayenne pepper
1 teaspoon dried tarragon
1 leaf fresh basil, chopped, *or* ¼ teaspoon dried
1 cup nonfat dry milk
2 cups water
Salt and freshly ground black pepper to taste
Paprika

Boil the sliced potatoes in their jackets until just tender. Heat the oil in a large nonstick skillet and brown the onion in it. Add the potatoes, then the watercress, parsley, stock, cumin, cayenne, tarragon, and basil. Cover and simmer 15 minutes. Add the milk mixed with water and simmer 1 minute more. Remove from heat, let cool, and turn into a food processor a little at a time and blend. Add salt and pepper to taste. Serve warm or chilled, with a dash of paprika for garnish. This soup will be tastier after refrigeration.

Makes 6 cups or 4 1½-cup servings

Per serving:	*Calcium* (mg)	*Fat* (g)	*Chol* (mg)	*Carbo* (g)	*Protein* (g)	*Calories*
	291	1.8	3	24.3	9.4	146

HOT PINK BORSCHT

¾ pound beets (makes about 3 cups)
1 cup peeled, seeded, and diced cucumber
2 cups buttermilk
1 tablespoon chopped onion
2 tablespoons fresh, chopped dill *or* 2 teaspoons dried
Dash dried thyme
Salt to taste
¼ teaspoon freshly ground pepper
1 cup plain low-fat or nonfat yogurt
2 tablespoons vinegar
1 teaspoon fresh lemon juice
Extra yogurt (optional)

Peel beets, cover with water, and boil until tender, about 30 minutes. Remove from water, cool, and chop fine. Reserve some of liquid to thin soup, if desired. Place cucumber, buttermilk, onion, herbs, and seasoning in food processor and puree. Add chopped beets, then the yogurt, vinegar, and lemon juice. Season again to taste. Serve cold garnished with dollop of yogurt, if desired.

Makes 6 cups or 6 1-cup servings

Per serving:	*Calcium* (mg)	*Fat* (g)	*Chol* (mg)	*Carbo* (g)	*Protein* (g)	*Calories*
	178	1.4	5	13.2	5.7	87

CONNIE'S IOWA BEAN SOUP

2 cups mixed dried beans, including limas, kidney and pinto beans, black-eyed and split peas, red lentils, navy beans, garbanzos, etc.
2 quarts water
2 tablespoons salt
2 chicken legs with thighs, skinned
4 tablespoons vinegar
1 large onion, chopped
1 28-ounce can Italian plum tomatoes, broken into pieces
Juice of 1 lemon
1 dried red pepper pod *or* 1 tablespoon seeded and chopped jalapeño pepper
Salt and freshly ground black pepper to taste
1 teaspoon Durkee's Imitation Bacon Bits

Place beans in large kettle, cover with water and 2 tablespoons salt, and let soak overnight. Replace water several times. When ready to cook, drain, place in the kettle with 2 quarts of water, and bring to boil. Add the chicken legs and vinegar, cover, and simmer slowly for 2½–3 hours. When beans are tender, remove chicken bones from the soup, leaving the meat, and add the onion, tomatoes, lemon juice, and red or jalapeño pepper. Cook, covered, for another 30 minutes. Add salt and pepper and the Bacon Bits, stir, and serve. A sturdy soup for a cool day, nice with salad and cheese for a light supper.

Makes 10 cups or 8 1¼-cup servings

Per serving:	*Calcium* (mg)	*Fat* (g)	*Chol* (mg)	*Carbo* (g)	*Protein* (g)	*Calories*
	31	1.7	22	17.2	13.8	137

MEXICAN CORN CHOWDER

1 teaspoon corn oil
1 cup chopped onion
1 clove garlic, minced
¼ cup chopped hot yellow pepper
½ cup chopped green bell pepper
1 cup diced tomatillos (Mexican green tomatoes) or regular green tomatoes
2 cups fresh corn kernels
2 cups Vegetable Stock (see index)
Salt and freshly ground black pepper to taste
2 cups skim milk
¼ cup diced red bell pepper

Heat oil in nonstick saucepan and cook onion and garlic in it until translucent. Add hot pepper, green pepper, green tomatoes, corn, and Vegetable Stock. Cook 10–15 minutes. Season with salt and pepper to taste. Remove about 1–1½ cups of the soup and puree in a food processor after cooling a bit. Return to soup pot and add the milk. Heat just to simmer. Pour into warm soup bowls and garnish each with diced red peppers.

Makes 6 cups or 6 1-cup servings

Per serving:	*Calcium* (mg)	*Fat* (g)	*Chol* (mg)	*Carbo* (g)	*Protein* (g)	*Calories*
	119	1.7	1.7	20.6	5.8	111

MUSHROOM AND BARLEY SOUP

3 dried black mushrooms (available in Oriental and health food stores)
1 teaspoon safflower oil
1 medium onion, chopped
2 cloves garlic, minced
1 pound mushrooms, sliced
½ cup raw barley
3 cups boiling Vegetable Stock (see index)
2 teaspoons low-sodium soy sauce
2 carrots, sliced
1 teaspoon dried dill weed
½ teaspoon dried thyme
Dash dried marjoram
2 cups skim milk plus 2 tablespoons nonfat dry milk
¼ teaspoon salt
Freshly ground pepper to taste
1 tablespoon chopped fresh parsley

Soften the dried mushrooms in a cup of boiling water for 20 minutes. Heat safflower oil in a large nonstick saucepan and cook onion and garlic in it until soft. Add sliced mushrooms and stir over low heat for 3 minutes. Drain the dried mushrooms, reserving the liquid (use for thinning soup later, if necessary). Rinse dried mushrooms under cold water, slice thin, and add to pot with remaining ingredients except the parsley. Cook over low heat for about an hour, until barley is tender. Sprinkle a little parsley over each serving.

Makes 7 cups or 7 1-cup servings

Per serving:	*Calcium* (mg)	*Fat* (g)	*Chol* (mg)	*Carbo* (g)	*Protein* (g)	*Calories*
	142	1.7	2	25.4	7.4	142

ORIENTAL SNOW PEA SOUP

4 cups Chicken Stock (see index)
5 ounces tofu (bean curd), cut into ½-inch cubes
¼ cup minced scallions
¼ cup thinly sliced mushrooms
¼ cup finely chopped carrots
1 clove garlic, minced
1 teaspoon grated fresh ginger
Pinch ground anise
1 teaspoon low-sodium soy sauce
1 cup snow peas, trimmed and washed
Extra scallions

Place all ingredients but the snow peas and extra scallions in a saucepan and bring to boil. Cover, reduce heat, and simmer until vegetables are tender, about 20 minutes. Add snow peas and cook another minute. Serve with garnish of scallions.

Makes 6 cups or 4 1½-cup servings

Per serving:	*Calcium* (mg)	*Fat* (g)	*Chol* (mg)	*Carbo* (g)	*Protein* (g)	*Calories*
	80	2.3	1	7.5	5.4	68

SALMON BISQUE

1 teaspoon vegetable oil
¼ cup chopped onion
½ cup chopped celery
¼ cup mashed boiled potato
2 cups skim milk
7 ounces canned pink salmon, with bones and liquid
1 tablespoon chopped fresh dill *or* ½ teaspoon dried
Dash cayenne pepper
Salt and freshly ground black pepper to taste
1 tablespoon chopped fresh parsley

Heat oil in nonstick saucepan and cook onions and celery in it until tender. Stir in potato and 1 cup milk and bring to boil. Add salmon and juice and the remaining milk, mashing the salmon well. Add dill, cayenne, and salt and pepper. Heat until slightly thick and adjust seasoning. Serve in bowls with garnish of fresh parsley. This is a substantial dish and is recommended as a main course, served with a good bread and salad.

Makes 5 cups or 4 1¼-cup servings

Per serving:	*Calcium* (mg)	*Fat* (g)	*Chol* (mg)	*Carbo* (g)	*Protein* (g)	*Calories*
	308	5.8	27	11.4	18.8	175

SHRIMP CHOWDER

¾ cup diced celery
3 tablespoons minced onion
1 clove garlic, minced
1 cup Chicken Stock or Vegetable Stock (see index)
2 4½-ounce cans tiny shrimp *or* 8 ounces fresh codfish, cut into chunks
½ cup nonfat dry milk
1½ cups water
1 cup diced cooked potato
1 tablespoon chopped fresh dill *or* ½ teaspoon dried
1 teaspoon curry powder (optional)
Salt and freshly ground pepper to taste

Place celery, onion, garlic, and stock in a saucepan and cook until vegetables are tender. Add remaining ingredients and heat. Season to taste.

Makes 5 cups or 4 1¼-cup servings

Per serving (using shrimp):	*Calcium* (mg)	*Fat* (g)	*Chol* (mg)	*Carbo* (g)	*Protein* (g)	*Calories*
	220	3.4	112	14.4	21.3	173

Per serving (using codfish):	*Calcium* (mg)	*Fat* (g)	*Chol* (mg)	*Carbo* (g)	*Protein* (g)	*Calories*
	160	5.5	5.5	14.2	21.3	193

SQUASH SOUP

2 acorn or butternut squash or pumpkin (equal to 3 cups pulp)
½ cup chopped onion
2 cups Chicken Stock (see index)
½ teaspoon ground cinnamon
¼ teaspoon ground coriander
¼ teaspoon ground cumin
⅛ teaspoon turmeric
Freshly ground pepper to taste
1 tablespoon apple cider vinegar
1 cup buttermilk
4 tablespoons nonfat dry milk
1 tablespoon low-sodium soy sauce
1 tablespoon chopped fresh parsley

Halve the squash or pumpkin and discard seeds. Slice and place in steamer basket over boiling water. Cover and steam about 20 minutes. Let cool and peel. There should be about 3 cups of pulp. Place pulp in a saucepan with the onion and Chicken Stock. Cook for 10 minutes, cool, then pour into a blender or food processor and puree. Return to saucepan and add the spices, vinegar, milks, and soy sauce. Bring to a gentle simmer. Adjust seasoning and serve in bowls with garnish of parsley.

Makes 6 cups or 6 1-cup servings

Per serving:	*Calcium* (mg)	*Fat* (g)	*Chol* (mg)	*Carbo* (g)	*Protein* (g)	*Calories*
	85	.7	2	12	3.3	62

SUMMER SOUP

½ cup peeled and diced potatoes
½ cup sliced carrots
½ cup chopped fresh spinach
½ cup fresh green peas
½ cup cauliflower florets
1 tablespoon arrowroot
1½ cups skim milk, divided
¼ teaspoon cayenne pepper
Salt and freshly ground black pepper to taste
1 tablespoon minced fresh parsley

In a medium saucepan, bring to boil 2 cups water with a pinch of salt and add the potatoes and carrots. Cover and cook 10 minutes. Add the remaining vegetables and cook another 5 minutes. In the meantime, make a paste of the arrowroot and 3 tablespoons of milk. Add to remaining milk and stir into the vegetables. Add cayenne and simmer another 5 minutes, until vegetables are tender. Season with salt and pepper to taste. Serve with garnish of fresh parsley.

Makes 4 cups or 4 1-cup servings

Per serving:	*Calcium* (mg)	*Fat* (g)	*Chol* (mg)	*Carbo* (g)	*Protein* (g)	*Calories*
	143	.4	2	16.9	5.6	90

TOMATO SHORBA

4 cups buttermilk
2 cups canned Italian plum tomatoes
1 tablespoon fresh lemon juice
2 tablespoons chopped scallion
1 tablespoon chopped fresh basil *or* 1 teaspoon dried
1 teaspoon curry powder
Dash white pepper
1 tablespoon chopped fresh parsley

Blend together all ingredients except parsley in a food processor. Serve cold with garnish of fresh parsley.

Makes 6 cups or 6 1-cup servings

Per serving:	*Calcium* (mg)	*Fat* (g)	*Chol* (mg)	*Carbo* (g)	*Protein* (g)	*Calories*
	200	1.6	6	12	6.3	86

TURKISH YOGURT SOUP

4 cups Chicken Stock (see index)
½ cup raw brown rice
Freshly ground pepper
1 cup plain low-fat yogurt
2 eggs (1 yolk only), beaten
1 tablespoon chopped fresh mint *or* 1 teaspoon dried, crushed
1 tablespoon minced fresh parsley

Bring Chicken Stock to boil in a saucepan and add the rice and pepper. Cover and simmer for 30 minutes or until rice is tender. Stir the yogurt into a bowl with the beaten eggs. To this add ¼ cup of the soup and mix. Then return this mixture to the soup in the saucepan and stir. Do not let this boil or the yogurt will separate. Serve garnished with dusting of mint and parsley.

Makes 6 cups or 6 1-cup servings

Per serving:	*Calcium* (mg)	*Fat* (g)	*Chol* (mg)	*Carbo* (g)	*Protein* (g)	*Calories*
	92	2.1	49	18	5.6	113

VICHYSSOISE

1 cup Chicken Stock (see index)
1 cup peeled and cubed potatoes
1½ cups chopped leeks washed well
2 cups skim milk
2 tablespoons nonfat dry milk
½ teaspoon salt
Dash freshly ground pepper
1 tablespoon part-skim ricotta cheese
1 tablespoon chopped chives

Pour stock, potatoes, and leeks into a food processor or blender and process, covered, to liquefy. Pour into a saucepan and cook until potatoes are tender. Place remaining ingredients except chives into blender, then add cooked vegetable mixture and process again until smooth. Pour into a bowl and chill before serving. Top with sprinkling of chives.

Makes 4 cups or 4 1-cup servings

Per serving:	*Calcium* (mg)	*Fat* (g)	*Chol* (mg)	*Carbo* (g)	*Protein* (g)	*Calories*
	233	2.9	11	19.2	7.7	133

ZUCCHINI SOUP

2 cups Vegetable Stock or Chicken Stock (see index)
2½ cups sliced zucchini
1 cup chopped onion
2 cloves garlic, minced
Dash dried marjoram
1 teaspoon curry powder
Salt and freshly ground black pepper to taste
2 tablespoons nonfat dry milk
1 cup plain low-fat yogurt
1 teaspoon fresh lemon juice
2 tablespoons diced red bell pepper or pimiento

Place all ingredients but last 3 in a medium saucepan and bring to boil. Reduce heat, skim off any froth that accumulates, cover, and simmer over low heat for 10 minutes or until zucchini is tender. Let cool, then puree in food processor, a little at a time. Add yogurt and lemon juice and chill well. Garnish with red pepper or pimiento.

Makes 6 cups or 4 1½-cup servings

Per serving:	*Calcium* (mg)	*Fat* (g)	*Chol* (mg)	*Carbo* (g)	*Protein* (g)	*Calories*
	155	1.3	4	11.2	5.5	76

3
ENTREES

Entrees are the mainstay of most meals, unless one is "grazing" and eating abundant smaller dishes. The main course recipes in this section are varied: some are vegetarian, some have meat, some fish or shellfish, but all of them are filling, delicious, easy to make, and a considerable calcium cache.

Calcium can be augmented by adding extra nonfat dry milk to favorite recipes such as chopped meat, turkey, and dairy dishes. Marinate fish or chicken in skim milk or buttermilk or yogurt before cooking. The best sources of calcium in the main dish department are low-fat cheeses; shellfish such as shrimp, scallops, oysters, and lobster; canned sardines and salmon with their bones; trout; "cream" sauces; sunflower and sesame seeds, almonds and hazelnuts; and tofu and other soybean products.

Many substitutions may be made in these recipes—chicken may be substituted for fish, or vice versa, and lobster for shrimp.

Meal plans should include an attractive combination of colors and textures, with vegetables and carbohydrates and greens providing balanced nutrition.

MEAT

GOAT-CHEESE BURGERS

1 pound 90-percent lean chopped round steak
½ teaspoon freshly ground pepper
½ teaspoon salt
1 tablespoon chopped onion
½ teaspoon ground coriander
4 tablespoons nonfat dry milk
2 tablespoons chopped fresh parsley
3 ounces goat cheese (in log shape, cut into 4 equal rounds)
Extra parsley for garnish

Mix all ingredients but goat cheese together with a fork, but do not overwork. Shape into 4 patties about ¾ inch thick. Grind a little extra pepper onto each side of them and place in preheated broiler about 3 inches from heat source. Broil for 3 minutes, turn, and broil other side for 2 minutes. Pull out broiler pan and top each burger with a goat cheese round. Return and broil for another 2 minutes, being careful not to let cheese burn. Remove and serve with garnish of parsley sprigs. Nice to serve with color-contrasting foods such as broiled tomatoes, snow peas, or asparagus.

Variation: This may be made with ground turkey rather than beef. It will then be lower in calories.

Serves 4

Per serving:	*Calcium* (mg)	*Fat* (g)	*Chol* (mg)	*Carbo* (g)	*Protein* (g)	*Calories*
	173	17.8	101	3.6	28.9	295

GREEN NOODLE MEAT CASSEROLE

7 ounces broad spinach or whole wheat noodles
¾ cup low-fat cottage cheese, rinsed under cold water
½ cup part-skim ricotta cheese
¼ cup minced onion
3 tablespoons chopped green bell pepper
1 tablespoon chopped fresh parsley
1 tablespoon drained and chopped pimiento
¾ pound 90-percent lean ground round steak
1 cup tomato sauce
1 tablespoon chopped fresh basil *or* 1 teaspoon dried
¼ teaspoon dried oregano
1 clove garlic, minced
½ teaspoon crushed hot red pepper
Salt and freshly ground black pepper
Vegetable spray

Cook the noodles according to package directions until just tender, drain, and set aside, keeping warm. Mix cottage cheese and ricotta and combine with chopped onion, green pepper, parsley, and pimiento. In a nonstick skillet, brown the meat. Drain off fat and liquid. Add tomato sauce to the meat along with basil, oregano, garlic, hot pepper, and salt and pepper. Stir to combine. Pour a small amount of the meat sauce into the bottom of a vegetable-sprayed 2-quart casserole or two loaf pans. Over the meat place half the noodles, then the cheese and vegetable mixture, then the remaining noodles, and top with the remaining meat sauce. Bake in preheated 350°F oven for 50 minutes.

Serves 6

Per serving:	*Calcium* (mg)	*Fat* (g)	*Chol* (mg)	*Carbo* (g)	*Protein* (g)	*Calories*
	109	9.8	7.3	25.5	22.6	284

LAMB KEBABS IN SPINACH SAUCE

2 tablespoons vegetable oil
3 tablespoons fresh lemon juice
¼ cup tarragon vinegar
1 tablespoon crushed garlic, divided
1 pound lean lamb, cubed, trimmed of fat
2 cups finely chopped cooked spinach (2 pounds fresh)
1 teaspoon minced onion
1 tablespoon grated fresh ginger (wash but do not peel)
1 cup plain low-fat yogurt
2 tablespoons nonfat dry milk

Make a marinade of the oil, lemon juice, vinegar, and half the garlic and marinate the lamb in it for 3 hours, turning to coat. Drain, then thread lamb cubes onto skewers and broil for 5 minutes, turning. In the meantime, heat the spinach in a saucepan and add the remaining garlic, the onion, and the ginger. Mix in the yogurt and the dry milk to make a sauce of medium thickness. Let heat, but do not boil. Remove lamb from skewers, pour sauce over meat, and serve. Nice with brown rice or sweet potatoes.

Serves 4

Per serving:	*Calcium* (mg)	*Fat* (g)	*Chol* (mg)	*Carbo* (g)	*Protein* (g)	*Calories*
	258	13.9	88	10.8	31.2	294

RICOTTA VEAL LOAF

1½ pounds lean ground veal
¼ cup nonfat dry milk
1 tablespoon chopped fresh parsley
1 small onion, chopped
1 clove garlic, minced
Salt and freshly ground pepper to taste
½ teaspoon dried oregano
½ teaspoon dried basil
¼ cup grated Parmesan or sapsago cheese
1 cup part-skim ricotta cheese
1 egg white, beaten

Preheat oven to 350°F. Mix together the veal, nonfat dry milk, parsley, onion, garlic, salt and pepper, herbs, and grated cheese. Blend the ricotta with the egg white. Place half the meat mixture into a loaf pan and spread the ricotta mixture over it. Top with remaining meat. Seal the edges to keep ricotta from escaping. Bake, uncovered, for 45 minutes.

Serves 8

Per serving:	*Calcium* (mg)	*Fat* (g)	*Chol* (mg)	*Carbo* (g)	*Protein* (g)	*Calories*
	137	9.8	76	3.2	22.5	197

VEGETABLE VEAL STEW

1 teaspoon safflower oil
1 cup coarsely chopped onion
2 cloves garlic, minced
1 pound stewing veal, cut into 1-inch cubes and trimmed of fat
2 tablespoons arrowroot
1½ cups Chicken Stock (see index)
¼ cup chopped fresh parsley
1 cup chopped carrot
½ pound mushrooms, sliced
1 bay leaf
½ teaspoon dried dill
1 teaspoon Hungarian sweet paprika
Salt and freshly ground pepper to taste
¼ cup dry white wine
1 cup plain low-fat yogurt

Heat oil in a nonstick saucepan and sauté onion and garlic in it. Add meat and brown. Remove meat and onions and keep warm. Stir arrowroot into the pan and cook until smooth. Add Chicken Stock and stir to blend. Return meat and onions to saucepan, add all remaining ingredients except yogurt, and cook until meat is tender, about 1½ hours. Adjust seasoning. Remove bay leaf, stir in yogurt, and heat until just warm. Stir and serve with brown rice pilaf or spinach noodles.

Serves 4

Per serving:	*Calcium* (mg)	*Fat* (g)	*Chol* (mg)	*Carbo* (g)	*Protein* (g)	*Calories*
	142	12.1	91	15.2	29	303

POULTRY

Chicken

CHICKEN A LA KING

1 teaspoon Best Butter (see index)
¼ cup chopped celery
1 cup sliced mushrooms
1½ cups Basic White Sauce (see index)
1 cup diced cooked chicken
¼ cup chopped and drained canned pimientos
¼ cup slivered blanched almonds
2 tablespoons dry sherry (optional)
Salt and freshly ground pepper
4 slices whole wheat toast, crusts trimmed, cut into triangles

Heat Best Butter in large nonstick skillet or saucepan and sauté the celery and mushrooms in it. Drain and set aside, keeping warm. Make the white sauce and then add to it the mushrooms, celery, chicken, and pimientos, stirring to combine. Add the almonds and sherry and adjust seasoning. Place toast triangles on warm plates and spoon the creamed chicken over them. Nice with a green vegetable such as broccoli or asparagus.

Serves 4

Per serving:	*Calcium* (mg)	*Fat* (g)	*Chol* (mg)	*Carbo* (g)	*Protein* (g)	*Calories*
	168	13.2	52	23.2	20.5	298

MOZZARELLA CHICKEN ROLLUPS

1 pound skinless and boneless chicken breasts, pounded flat
Salt
1 teaspoon Dijon mustard
4 large or 8 small leaves fresh sage
4 ounces part-skim mozzarella cheese, cut into 4 slices
1 teaspoon safflower oil
½ cup chopped onion
1 cup sliced mushrooms
Freshly ground pepper
1 tablespoon chopped fresh parsley
¼ cup dry white wine

Preheat oven to 350°F. Trim chicken breasts of all fat and sprinkle with a little salt. Spread ¼ teaspoon mustard on each. Place 1 large or 2 small sage leaves and 1 slice of the cheese on each. Roll up to make little bundles and seal edges with small skewer or toothpicks. Heat the oil in a nonstick skillet and cook onions until translucent. Brown chicken rolls lightly. Transfer to a baking dish and top with mushrooms, pepper, parsley, and wine. Cover and bake for 30 minutes.

Serves 4

Per serving:	*Calcium* (mg)	*Fat* (g)	*Chol* (mg)	*Carbo* (g)	*Protein* (g)	*Calories*
	205	9.1	82	4	32.3	243

MURGI CHICKEN CURRY

1 tablespoon vegetable oil
2 large onions, chopped
2 cloves garlic, minced
5 teaspoons good curry powder
1 pound skinless and boneless chicken breasts, cut up
1½ cups plain low-fat yogurt
2 tomatoes, seeded and chopped

Heat oil in large nonstick skillet and sauté onions and garlic in it. Stir in curry powder. Brown chicken pieces in skillet. Mix in the yogurt and add the tomatoes. Bring to boil, then lower heat and cook gently until chicken is tender, about 10 minutes. Serve over brown rice or boiled potatoes with a cucumber-sprout or green pepper vegetable dish.

Serves 4

Per serving:	*Calcium* (mg)	*Fat* (g)	*Chol* (mg)	*Carbo* (g)	*Protein* (g)	*Calories*
	192	8	71	14.8	30.8	258

SAUTEED CHICKEN WITH YOGURT

1 tablespoon vegetable oil
1 pound boneless and skinless chicken breasts, all fat removed
1 small onion, minced
1 clove garlic, minced
1 tablespoon arrowroot
1 cup evaporated skim milk
½ cup water
½ teaspoon freshly grated nutmeg
Salt and freshly ground pepper to taste
1½ cups plain low-fat yogurt
2 tablespoons finely chopped fresh parsley

Heat oil in a nonstick skillet and sauté chicken in it until lightly browned. Remove chicken and keep warm. In same pan, cook onion and garlic until translucent, then add the arrowroot and cook over low heat, stirring. Remove from heat. Mix evaporated skim milk and water and add to the skillet gradually, stirring with a whisk. Return to heat and continue stirring. Cook for a minute, until the sauce has reached a boil. Season with nutmeg and salt and pepper. Stir in yogurt. Add sautéed chicken and simmer over low heat, covered, 45 minutes. Serve with garnish of chopped parsley.

Serves 4

Per serving:	*Calcium* (mg)	*Fat* (g)	*Chol* (mg)	*Carbo* (g)	*Protein* (g)	*Calories*
	183	8.1	72	10	29.7	238

SPINACH CHICKEN BAKE

4 medium red potatoes (about 1 pound)
1 pound skinless and boneless chicken breasts, cut into 4 pieces
1 tablespoon oil
½ cup chopped onion
1 clove garlic, minced
1 pound fresh spinach, trimmed, steamed, drained, and chopped
¼ teaspoon freshly grated nutmeg
Vegetable spray
1 cup plain low-fat yogurt
2 tablespoons fresh lemon juice
½ teaspoon salt
Freshly ground pepper to taste
1 tablespoon chopped fresh parsley

Wash but do not peel potatoes. Cut them into bite-sized pieces and boil in saucepan until tender but still firm. Meanwhile, brown the chicken cutlets in a nonstick skillet in 1 tablespoon of oil. Remove when browned and set aside. Sauté onion and garlic in same skillet. Blend the spinach with the onions and garlic and stir in nutmeg. Drain the potatoes and combine with spinach mixture. Coat a large casserole with vegetable spray and turn the mixture into it. Arrange the chicken on top. Mix the yogurt with lemon juice, salt, and pepper and spoon over the chicken. Sprinkle with parsley, cover, and bake 45 minutes in preheated 350°F oven.

Serves 4

Per serving:	*Calcium* (mg)	*Fat* (g)	*Chol* (mg)	*Carbo* (g)	*Protein* (g)	*Calories*
	230	4.7	70	22.4	33	260

Turkey

TURKEY DIVAN

2 cups cut-up fresh broccoli
1 tablespoon Best Butter (see index)
1 tablespoon arrowroot
2 tablespoons minced onion
1 cup skim milk
1 tablespoon dry sherry
½ teaspoon Dijon mustard
⅛ teaspoon cayenne pepper
½ cup grated part-skim mozzarella cheese
1 teaspoon minced fresh parsley
2 cups cubed cooked turkey breast
2 tablespoons grated Parmesan or sapsago cheese

Blanch broccoli, drain, and arrange in bottom of ovenproof casserole. In a saucepan, heat Best Butter and add arrowroot. Cook about 1 minute, then add onion and cook over low heat. Mix the milk with sherry, mustard, and cayenne. Gradually add to saucepan, stirring until slightly thickened. Add grated mozzarella cheese and parsley and cook until the cheese melts. Add turkey and blend thoroughly. Pour mixture over the broccoli, sprinkle with grated Parmesan, and bake in preheated 350°F oven until top is brown and bubbling, about 35 minutes. Nice with spinach noodles.

Serves 6

Per serving:	*Calcium* (mg)	*Fat* (g)	*Chol* (mg)	*Carbo* (g)	*Protein* (g)	*Calories*
	200	7.2	65	8.3	30.6	222

TURKEY STROGANOFF

1 pound ground turkey
1 teaspoon vegetable oil
½ cup minced onion
2 cloves garlic, minced
2 cups sliced mushrooms (about ½ pound)
2 tablespoons arrowroot
¾ cup chicken broth
¾ cup red wine
½ teaspoon salt
Pinch Hungarian sweet paprika
1 teaspoon poppy seeds
1 cup low-fat plain yogurt

In a large nonstick skillet, brown the turkey, then remove, drain, and reserve. In same pan, heat the oil, add onion and garlic to soften, add mushrooms, and cook until soft. Stir in the arrowroot, then the broth and wine. Bring to simmer and stir until sauce thickens. Add salt, paprika, and poppy seeds and mix. Return turkey to the skillet and simmer about 5 minutes. Remove from heat, stir in yogurt, and serve with potatoes, rice, or noodles.

Serves 4

Per serving:	*Calcium* (mg)	*Fat* (g)	*Chol* (mg)	*Carbo* (g)	*Protein* (g)	*Calories*
	134	10	64	13.8	30.1	308

SEAFOOD

BAKED BLUEFISH DULSE

Vegetable spray
1½ pounds bluefish fillets
1 cup Yogurt Sour Cream (see note below)
1 tablespoon low-sodium soy sauce
⅓ cup minced green onions
1 teaspoon grated fresh ginger (washed but unpeeled)
1 teaspoon Dijon mustard
2 tablespoons dulse or nori (or any dried seaweed available in health food stores or Oriental markets)
1 tablespoon chopped fresh parsley

Preheat oven to 450°F. With vegetable spray, coat a baking dish large enough to hold fish. Wash and pat dry the fish fillets and place in baking dish. Mix remaining ingredients except the seaweed and parsley and spread over the fish. Bake, uncovered, on highest rack for 10–15 minutes. Toast seaweed by passing it over stove top burner, then crumble it. Garnish fish with sprinkling of the toasted seaweed and chopped parsley.

Note: To make 1 cup plain Yogurt Sour Cream, follow recipe for Yogurt Sour Cream (see index), using 2 cups plain nonfat or low-fat yogurt.

Serves 4

Per serving:	*Calcium* (mg)	*Fat* (g)	*Chol* (mg)	*Carbo* (g)	*Protein* (g)	*Calories*
	176	3.4	58	7.4	26.8	193

INDIAN FISH BAKE

¼ cup nonfat dry milk
2 cups hot mashed potatoes
Vegetable spray
1 cup plain low-fat yogurt
1 pound (2 cups) flaked, cold, cooked fish such as cod, haddock, or snapper
1 green chili, minced
1 small onion, minced
1 tablespoon minced fresh parsley or watercress
½ teaspoon salt
Dash freshly ground pepper
Paprika
¼ cup chopped chives

Mash the dry milk into the potatoes, adding water to thin, if necessary, then turn half the mixture into a vegetable-sprayed casserole. Mix the yogurt with the fish, chili, onion, parsley, and salt and pepper. Spread over the potatoes. Top with remaining potatoes. Sprinkle with paprika and bake in preheated 350°F oven for 15 minutes, until top is browned. Sprinkle chives over top and serve.

Serves 4

Per serving:	*Calcium* (mg)	*Fat* (g)	*Chol* (mg)	*Carbo* (g)	*Protein* (g)	*Calories*
	217	9.9	87	21.3	31.4	303

CRAB GRATIN

Vegetable spray
2 tablespoons Best Butter (see index)
2 tablespoons minced shallots
½ pound lump or backfin crabmeat, picked over
Salt and freshly ground pepper
¼ teaspoon dried tarragon, crushed
⅓ cup dry vermouth
½ cup evaporated skim milk
1 tablespoon arrowroot
4 tablespoons nonfat dry milk
½ teaspoon tomato paste
Dash fresh lemon juice
2 tablespoons grated Parmesan or sapsago cheese
Paprika

Coat 4 scallop shells or 1 8-inch gratin dish with vegetable spray. Heat Best Butter in a nonstick skillet and cook shallots in it. Add crab, salt, pepper, and tarragon and cook for 2 minutes, stirring. Add vermouth, turn up heat and boil, stirring, until liquid has nearly evaporated. Remove from heat. In a small bowl, mix 3 tablespoons of evaporated skim milk with the arrowroot and beat in remaining milk, nonfat dry milk, and tomato paste. Add to crab mixture and return to moderate heat. Bring to simmer and cook about 2 minutes, stirring. If sauce is too thick, add a little more milk. Adjust seasoning and add dash of lemon juice. Spoon crab mixture into the shells or gratin dish and sprinkle tops with grated cheese. Sprinkle with paprika and place under broiler for 5 minutes, until cheese browns. Remove and serve with a simple bread and salad.

Serves 4

Per serving:	*Calcium* (mg)	*Fat* (g)	*Chol* (mg)	*Carbo* (g)	*Protein* (g)	*Calories*
	163	8.7	96	10.8	19	231

LOBSTER NEWBURG

1 tablespoon Best Butter (see index)
1 tablespoon arrowroot
1½ cups evaporated skim milk
2 cups cooked lobster meat (see Chapter 12) (2 1½-pound lobsters)
½ teaspoon salt
Dash white pepper
¼ teaspoon paprika
¼ teaspoon freshly grated nutmeg
2 tablespoons dry sherry
¼ cup chopped fresh parsley

Heat Best Butter in nonstick saucepan and add arrowroot, stirring for a few minutes until blended. Add the milk, stir, and cook until smooth. Add lobster pieces, spices, and sherry and cook until just thickened. Serve over brown rice or noodles with garnish of chopped parsley.

Serves 4

Per serving:	*Calcium* (mg)	*Fat* (g)	*Chol* (mg)	*Carbo* (g)	*Protein* (g)	*Calories*
	74	3.8	41	5.8	10.6	104

QUICK OYSTER STEW

16 fresh oysters
¼ cup clam juice
2 tablespoons whipped butter
2 dashes celery salt
2 teaspoons low-sodium soy sauce
1 cup skim milk
1 cup evaporated skim milk
Paprika
1 teaspoon chopped fresh parsley
Freshly ground pepper (optional)

Heat 2 soup bowls before starting this quick dish. Make certain oysters are fresh; they should be tightly closed when purchased. Shuck oysters (see Chapter 12) and reserve liquid from them. Place the oysters, ½ cup reserved oyster liquid, clam juice, butter, celery salt, and soy sauce in the top of a double boiler set over boiling water. Stir briskly for 1 minute until oysters plump up and edges begin to curl. Add the skim milk and evaporated skim milk, stir briskly, and remove from heat just before liquid reaches the boil. Ladle into the hot bowls and garnish each with a dusting of paprika and parsley. Season with pepper if desired. Serve with plain oyster crackers.

Serves 2

Per serving:	*Calcium* (mg)	*Fat* (g)	*Chol* (mg)	*Carbo* (g)	*Protein* (g)	*Calories*
	216	12.1	91	10.5	15.1	212

CONFETTI SALMON MOUSSE

1 envelope plain gelatin
½ cup boiling water
2 tablespoons fresh lemon juice
½ cup chopped onion
¼ teaspoon paprika
1 tablespoon chopped fresh dill *or* 1 teaspoon dried
2 dashes cayenne pepper
1 cup nonfat or low-fat plain yogurt
2 cups canned pink salmon with skin and bones, drained
¼ cup diced red and green bell peppers
2 cups fresh spinach leaves, romaine, or other salad greens
½ cup alfalfa sprouts

Pour gelatin powder into food processor and add boiling water, lemon juice, onion, paprika, dill, and cayenne and puree for 1 minute. Add yogurt and mix until just blended. Mash salmon and bones and stir into yogurt mix. Scatter the mixed red and green peppers around the bottom of a ring mold and pour salmon mixture into the mold. Chill until ready to serve. To unmold, place form in a hot water bath for a minute or so and then turn onto a platter lined with greens. Place alfalfa sprouts in center. Serve with sliced tomatoes and cucumbers if desired.

Makes 4 cups or 4 1-cup servings

Per serving:	*Calcium* (mg)	*Fat* (g)	*Chol* (mg)	*Carbo* (g)	*Protein* (g)	*Calories*
	355	7.5	42	9	27.4	215

POACHED SALMON WITH HORSERADISH

1 small onion, quartered
6 black peppercorns
1 bay leaf
2 slices lemon
1 pound salmon fillets, cut into 4 slices
¼ cup minced fresh dill
¼ cup freshly grated horseradish
Freshly ground pepper to taste
1 teaspoon fresh lime juice
1 teaspoon Dijon mustard
1 cup plain low-fat yogurt
Parsley or dill sprigs

Fill a large, deep skillet with 2 inches of water, bring to boil, and add onion, peppercorns, bay leaf, and lemon. Let boil 5 minutes. Lower heat to the simmer and slide in the salmon fillets. Cover and poach gently for 5 minutes. Remove from bouillon (save it as fish stock, strained, for later use). Chill the fish before serving. In the meantime, combine the remaining ingredients except parsley or dill sprigs and set aside for 30 minutes or more. When ready to serve, spoon some of the sauce onto the serving plate and place salmon over it. Serve rest of sauce separately. Garnish with parsley or a sprig of dill.

Note: Other fish fillets such as mackerel, bluefish, or swordfish may be substituted.

Serves 4

Per serving:	*Calcium* (mg)	*Fat* (g)	*Chol* (mg)	*Carbo* (g)	*Protein* (g)	*Calories*
	335	7.4	42	7.3	26.2	205

SALMON CROQUETTES

1½ cups canned pink salmon, with the bones
3 cups peeled and cooked potatoes (about 1 pound), mashed
¼ cup diced green bell pepper
2 tablespoons minced scallions
½ teaspoon paprika
1 egg white, beaten
Dash cayenne pepper
½ teaspoon dried dill weed
½ teaspoon mustard
Freshly ground black pepper to taste
¼ cup wheat germ
1 tablespoon vegetable oil
Mushroom Cream Sauce (see index)
Chopped fresh parsley

Mash together first 10 ingredients and shape into croquettes or patties. Spread wheat germ on flat surface and roll croquettes in it until coated. Heat oil in nonstick skillet and brown croquettes in it on all sides. Serve with 1 tablespoon Mushroom Cream Sauce per patty and sprinkling of parsley.

Makes about 10 patties or 5 2-patty servings

	Calcium (mg)	*Fat* (g)	*Chol* (mg)	*Carbo* (g)	*Protein* (g)	*Calories*
Per patty:	99	7.5	21	11.4	10.4	150

SALMON LOAF EVELYN

½ cup quick oats
15 ounces canned pink salmon with bones, drained
4 tablespoons plain low-fat or nonfat yogurt
1 teaspoon fresh lemon juice
1 tablespoon minced onion
1 tablespoon chopped fresh dill *or* 1 teaspoon dried
Few dashes cayenne pepper
Vegetable spray
6 pimiento-stuffed olives, sliced
3 tablespoons Grape Nuts

Mix together all ingredients except vegetable spray, olives, and Grape Nuts. Coat a loaf pan with vegetable spray, then line with olive slices. Turn salmon mixture into pan, sprinkle Grape Nuts on top, and bake, covered, in a preheated 400°F oven for 30 minutes. Turn out onto platter to serve.

Serves 4

Per serving:	*Calcium* (mg)	*Fat* (g)	*Chol* (mg)	*Carbo* (g)	*Protein* (g)	*Calories*
	258	.6	39	15.6	26.7	242

SALMON-STUFFED PEPPERS

15 ounces canned pink salmon with bones, drained
1 cup shredded low-fat cheddar cheese or Formagg
¼ cup grated sapsago or Romano cheese
3 medium green bell peppers
3 medium red bell peppers
1 teaspoon vegetable oil
1 cup minced onion
1 clove garlic, chopped
1½ cups drained and chopped canned Italian plum tomatoes
1 teaspoon dried oregano, crumbled
¼ teaspoon freshly ground black pepper
Dash cayenne pepper
2 tablespoons raw wheat germ

Combine drained salmon and bones with the cheeses. Trim tops off peppers and remove seeds and rough white ribs. Chop end pieces of peppers and add to oiled nonstick skillet along with the onion and garlic. Cook until tender and add tomatoes, oregano, and black and cayenne peppers. Cook for 2 minutes, mixing well. Add to salmon and cheese mixture. Stuff the peppers, top with sprinkling of wheat germ, and stand them up in ovenproof casserole, adding about ¼ cup of water. Cover with foil and bake in preheated 350°F oven for 30–40 minutes.

Serves 6

Per serving:	*Calcium* (mg)	*Fat* (g)	*Chol* (mg)	*Carbo* (g)	*Protein* (g)	*Calories*
	389	8.4	53	13.3	25.4	277

COQUILLES ST. JACQUES

1 cup Chicken Stock (see index)
2 scallions, sliced
5 peppercorns
2 cups bay scallops (1 pound)
3 tablespoons dry vermouth or sherry
2 tablespoons arrowroot
2 tablespoons nonfat dry milk
½ cup buttermilk
1 teaspoon fresh lemon juice
Dash cayenne pepper
Vegetable spray
1 cup sliced mushrooms (½ pound)
½ cup grated low-fat cheese (skim-milk mozzarella or Muenster)
1 tablespoon wheat germ
2 tablespoons chopped fresh parsley

In a saucepan, bring stock to simmer with scallions and peppercorns and cook for 10 minutes. Strain and return liquid to pot. Add scallops and cook, covered, for 1–2 minutes. Remove scallops and keep warm. Add vermouth or sherry to the saucepan and boil down to 1 cup. In the meantime, in a bowl, mix together arrowroot, dry milk, and buttermilk. Slowly add to stock sauce with lemon juice and cayenne. Coat scallop shells or casserole with vegetable spray and spoon into them equal portions of mushrooms and scallops, covering each with the sauce. Top with grated cheese and wheat germ. Place shells on cookie sheet and bake in preheated 350°F oven for 10 minutes. Then quickly pass under broiler to brown. Garnish with chopped parsley.

Serves 4

Per serving:	*Calcium* (mg)	*Fat* (g)	*Chol* (mg)	*Carbo* (g)	*Protein* (g)	*Calories*
	349	5.5	79	13.6	36.2	255

RED AND GREEN SCALLOP DELIGHT

1 pound large sea scallops
1½ cups tomato sauce
1 teaspoon (or less) crushed hot red pepper
1 clove garlic, minced
½ teaspoon minced fresh ginger
1 tablespoon chopped green bell pepper
2 scallions, chopped
3 cups fresh broccoli florets
2 cups quartered fresh tomatoes
Chopped fresh parsley

Slice scallops in half horizontally. Heat tomato sauce in large skillet and add hot red pepper, garlic, ginger, green pepper, and scallions. Stir to combine. Blanch the broccoli, remove from pot, and drain. Drop scallops and tomatoes into the cooked sauce and stir, cooking about 3–5 minutes. Arrange broccoli around outer rim of a deep serving dish and spoon scallops with sauce into the middle of the plate. Garnish with parsley.

Serves 4

Per serving:	*Calcium* (mg)	*Fat* (g)	*Chol* (mg)	*Carbo* (g)	*Protein* (g)	*Calories*
	260	12.6	78	28.2	41.5	363

SCALLOP AND OYSTER SALAD

1 teaspoon minced shallot
1 tablespoon wine vinegar
Salt and freshly ground white pepper to taste
¼ teaspoon mustard
3 tablespoons fresh lemon juice
1 tablespoon olive oil
2 cups loosely packed, shredded spinach, well washed and spun dry (about ½ pound fresh spinach leaves)
1 cup finely shredded radicchio or red leaf lettuce
2 small tomatoes, peeled, seeded, and cut into ½-inch pieces
10 fresh sea scallops, rinsed, dried, and sliced in half
12 fresh oysters, shucked (see Chapter 12)
1 tablespoon chopped fresh parsley

Combine the shallot, vinegar, salt, pepper, mustard, and lemon juice in a small bowl. Slowly stir in oil until blended. Toss the spinach with half the dressing and place on 4 salad plates. Toss the radicchio with remaining dressing and arrange over spinach. Place the tomato pieces on top of the spinach in 4 little mounds. Broil the scallops for 2 minutes, turning to cook on both sides. Set a steamer basket over boiling water and steam the oysters, covered, for just 1 minute, until their edges curl and they are just heated but not cooked. Remove and arrange both scallops and oysters decoratively on the 4 plates. Sprinkle tops with garnish of chopped parsley and a dash of white pepper. Nice with a good bread for a light supper or luncheon.

Serves 4

Per serving:	*Calcium* (mg)	*Fat* (g)	*Chol* (mg)	*Carbo* (g)	*Protein* (g)	*Calories*
	258	12	58	11.7	24.8	240

CURRIED SHRIMP AND SCALLOPS

1 small onion, chopped
½ cup chopped green pepper
Vegetable oil
1 tablespoon Best Butter (see index)
1 tablespoon arrowroot
1 cup evaporated skim milk
2 tablespoons nonfat dry milk
2 teaspoons curry powder
2 tablespoons dry white wine (optional)
½ pound medium shrimp, cooked, peeled, and deveined
½ pound sea scallops, sliced in half
½ cup seeded and chopped fresh tomato
2 tablespoons slivered almonds
1 tablespoon chopped fresh parsley

In a nonstick skillet, sauté the onion and green pepper in a little oil. Remove from pan and reserve. Heat Best Butter in skillet and blend in arrowroot. Add evaporated milk and dry milk, and stir until sauce thickens. Add curry, wine, shrimp, scallops, sautéed vegetables, and chopped tomatoes, and heat through. Serve over hot brown rice with a garnish of almonds and parsley.

Serves 4

Per serving:	*Calcium* (mg)	*Fat* (g)	*Chol* (mg)	*Carbo* (g)	*Protein* (g)	*Calories*
	255	6.9	112	17.4	34.4	209

GREEN AND WHITE FISH ROLLS

1 tablespoon Best Butter (see index), divided
2 tablespoons minced shallots
1 pound sole or flounder fillets
20 green beans or thin asparagus spears
Vegetable spray
1 tablespoon arrowroot
1 cup skim milk
2 tablespoons grated sharp cheddar cheese (½ ounce) or Formagg
Salt and freshly ground black pepper to taste
Dash cayenne pepper
2 tablespoons grated Parmesan cheese
Paprika
Chopped fresh parsley

In nonstick skillet, heat 1 teaspoon of Best Butter and sauté shallots in it. Wash fish fillets and pat dry. Spread browned shallots over fillets. In the meantime, blanch beans or asparagus, drain, and place in equal portions in center of fillets. Roll up around vegetables and secure with toothpicks or small skewers. Coat baking dish with vegetable spray and arrange the rolled fillets in dish.

Melt remaining 2 teaspoons Best Butter in a saucepan and stir in arrowroot, blending well. Stir in milk and, when sauce begins to thicken, add cheddar cheese, salt, pepper, and cayenne. Spoon sauce over the fish fillets, then top with the Parmesan and a sprinkle of paprika. Bake, uncovered, in preheated 350°F oven for 15 minutes or until cheese sauce is bubbly. Run under broiler to brown. Remove, garnish with parsley, and serve.

Serves 4

Per serving:	*Calcium* (mg)	*Fat* (g)	*Chol* (mg)	*Carbo* (g)	*Protein* (g)	*Calories*
	174	10	86	7.7	31.1	251

SOLE FLORENTINE

½ pound fresh spinach, steamed and chopped
½ cup part-skim ricotta cheese
½ cup low-fat cottage cheese
4 tablespoons nonfat dry milk
2 tablespoons chopped fresh parsley, divided
¼ teaspoon freshly grated nutmeg
½ teaspoon salt
Dash freshly ground pepper
8 medium sole or flounder fillets (about 1 pound)
Vegetable spray
2 tablespoons grated Parmesan or sapsago cheese
Paprika

Press all excess moisture from the spinach and mix with ricotta, cottage cheese, nonfat dry milk, 1 tablespoon of parsley, and seasonings. Place a generous 2 tablespoons of this filling in the center of each fish fillet. Roll up and fold ends of fish together and place seam side down, arranged snugly side by side, in a vegetable-sprayed baking dish. Sprinkle with Parmesan or sapsago and garnish with ribbon of remaining parsley and dash of paprika. Bake 45 minutes in preheated 350°F oven.

Serves 4

Per serving:	*Calcium* (mg)	*Fat* (g)	*Chol* (mg)	*Carbo* (g)	*Protein* (g)	*Calories*
	210	10.6	91	5	35.4	260

PIZZA, PASTA, AND VEGETABLE PIES

PIZZA PANOPLY

Basic Pizza Dough

1¼ teaspoons active dry yeast
⅔ cup warm (105–115°F) water
2 tablespoons vegetable oil
¾ teaspoon coarse salt
3 tablespoons nonfat dry milk
¾ cup whole wheat flour
1–1¼ cups all-purpose unbleached flour
Vegetable oil for bowl

Dissolve the yeast in ⅔ cup warm water and let stand 5 minutes, until it bubbles. Stir in the 2 tablespoons of vegetable oil, the salt, the dry milk, then the whole wheat flour until blended. Gradually add unbleached flour to make a rough dough. Turn out on floured surface and knead for about 4 minutes, adding more unbleached flour as necessary to make a soft dough. Lightly oil a bowl and place the dough in it, turning to coat all sides. Cover and place in draft-free warm place for about 3–4 hours, until dough has tripled in bulk. Punch down dough and roll out on floured surface to form a 12-inch circle. Top with any of the following fillings.

Note: Dough may be allowed to rise for 2 hours, punched down, and refrigerated or frozen, tightly wrapped. When ready to use again, remove from freezer, let thaw, unwrap, and let rise for 2 hours in a warm place; then proceed as in basic recipe.

Serves 6

Per serving (crust only):	*Calcium* (mg)	*Fat* (g)	*Chol* (mg)	*Carbo* (g)	*Protein* (g)	*Calories*
	38	5.8	0	29.6	5.4	190

Ratatouille Topping

1 teaspoon olive oil
½ cup chopped onion
1 clove garlic, minced
½ cup diced eggplant
½ cup chopped zucchini
1 medium ripe tomato, peeled, seeded, and chopped (about 1 cup)
2 tablespoons minced fresh parsley
1 tablespoon chopped fresh basil *or* 1 teaspoon dried
1 teaspoon dried oregano
Salt and freshly ground pepper to taste
½ cup grated part-skim mozzarella cheese

Heat oil in nonstick skillet and sauté onion and garlic in it. Add eggplant and zucchini and cook about 5 minutes. Add tomato, herbs, and salt and pepper, and cook until vegetables are tender. Spread over a 12-inch pizza crust. Spread mozzarella over the vegetable layer and bake in preheated 400°F oven about 25–30 minutes.

Serves 6

Per serving (topping only):	*Calcium* (mg)	*Fat* (g)	*Chol* (mg)	*Carbo* (g)	*Protein* (g)	*Calories*
	113	8.1	6	32.9	8.4	134

Shrimp and Leek Topping

¼ cup Vegetable Stock (see index)
2 cups thinly sliced leeks, well washed
2 tablespoons grated Parmesan or sapsago cheese
1 large ripe tomato, peeled, seeded, and diced
¼ pound medium shrimp, shelled and deveined

Bring Vegetable Stock to simmer and lightly cook leeks in it. Sprinkle grated Parmesan or sapsago over pizza crust, then top with drained leeks and tomato. Bake 15–20 minutes in preheated 400°F oven, remove from oven, and arrange shrimp on top. Bake 5 minutes more, until the shrimp turn pink and are cooked through.

Serves 6

Per serving (topping only):	*Calcium* (mg)	*Fat* (g)	*Chol* (mg)	*Carbo* (g)	*Protein* (g)	*Calories*
	171	9.4	14	37.5	9.5	269

Mozzarella, Tomato, and Sardine Topping

2 cups peeled, seeded, and diced tomatoes
1 8-ounce can sardines in tomato sauce
4 ounces part-skim mozzarella, grated
2 tablespoons grated Parmesan or sapsago cheese

Arrange tomatoes over pizza crust, top with the sardines and sauce, then spread on the mozzarella and sprinkle with Parmesan. Bake 25–30 minutes in preheated 400°F oven.

Serves 6

Per serving (topping only):	*Calcium* (mg)	*Fat* (g)	*Chol* (mg)	*Carbo* (g)	*Protein* (g)	*Calories*
	290	12	46	33.1	17.2	307

PASTA

FLORENTINE LASAGNA ROLLUPS

12 ripple-edged lasagna noodles
1 tablespoon vegetable oil
¾ cup chopped onion
2 10-ounce packages frozen chopped spinach, thawed and drained
½ teaspoon freshly grated nutmeg
½ teaspoon salt
Freshly ground pepper to taste
½ cup plain low-fat yogurt
4 ounces shredded part-skim mozzarella cheese
1 tablespoon Best Butter (see index)
1 tablespoon arrowroot
1 cup evaporated skim milk
½ cup skim milk
2 teaspoons Vogue Instant Chicken Flavored Base
¼ cup grated Parmesan or sapsago cheese

Preheat oven to 350°F. Cook the lasagna noodles in boiling water according to package directions until just tender (usually about 12 minutes). Drain and set aside, flat. Heat oil in a nonstick skillet and sauté onions in it. Combine with the spinach, spices, yogurt, and mozzarella and set aside. In the meantime, melt Best Butter in a saucepan, add the arrowroot, and cook about 1 minute, stirring until smooth. Pour in evaporated milk and skim milk and blend until creamy (see directions for Basic White Sauce).

Add the Chicken Flavored Base and stir until dissolved. Remove from heat. Spread a little of the sauce in a 9- by 13-inch baking dish. Then spoon about ¼ cup of the spinach mixture on each lasagna noodle and roll up in jelly roll fashion. Place filled noodles alongside each other in the baking dish. Pour remaining sauce on top and sprinkle with the cheese. Bake for 30–35 minutes, until hot and bubbly.

Serves 6 (two per person)

Per rollup:	Calcium (mg)	Fat (g)	Chol (mg)	Carbo (g)	Protein (g)	Calories
	174	4.7	9	21.4	8.2	159

TOFU SOBA NOODLE BAKE

8 ounces buckwheat soba noodles *or* 2 cups cooked Basic Brown Rice (see index)
Vegetable spray
1 teaspoon safflower oil
½ cup chopped onion
2 cloves garlic
¼ cup chopped fresh parsley, divided
½ teaspoon grated fresh ginger
½ cup chopped red bell pepper
1 cup chopped bok choy
8 ounces tofu (bean curd), drained and mashed
¼ cup Ricotta Peanut Butter (see index)
1 teaspoon slivered lemon zest

Cook soba noodles in boiling water until tender (only 3–5 minutes). Drain and turn into a vegetable-sprayed 1½-quart casserole. Heat the oil in a nonstick skillet and sauté the onion in it. Mince the garlic together with 2 tablespoons of parsley and add to skillet with ginger. Add red pepper and bok choy and cook a few minutes, stirring to combine. Add mashed tofu and blend. Place the tofu and vegetable mixture over the noodles and top with Ricotta Peanut Butter. Bake in preheated 350°F oven for about 25 minutes. Remove from oven, top with remaining parsley, and garnish with lemon zest.

Serves 4

Per serving:	Calcium (mg)	Fat (g)	Chol (mg)	Carbo (g)	Protein (g)	Calories
	173	10.8	34	31.6	15.1	273

MUSHROOM MANICOTTI

6 manicotti shells
1 pound fresh spinach
1 tablespoon vegetable oil
1 small onion, chopped fine
1 clove garlic, minced
6 ounces fresh mushrooms, rinsed and sliced
1 egg white
1 cup part-skim ricotta cheese
¾ cup grated part-skim mozzarella cheese
2 tablespoons grated Parmesan or sapsago cheese
½ teaspoon freshly grated nutmeg
½ teaspoon salt
Dash freshly ground pepper
Vegetable spray
3 ounces tomato paste
1 cup water
Pinch each dried basil, thyme, oregano, and rosemary

Preheat oven to 375°F. Cook manicotti shells as directed on package, for about 10–12 minutes, until tender, then drain. Wash the spinach well, trim, and then steam. Drain and chop fine. Heat oil in a nonstick skillet and lightly sauté onions and garlic in it. Add mushrooms and cook until liquid is released. Drain. Beat the egg white until stiff but not dry. In a separate bowl, mix ricotta, mozzarella (reserving some for topping), Parmesan or sapsago, spinach, sautéed vegetables, and spices. Fold egg white into ricotta mixture. Stuff the shells and place in a vegetable-sprayed baking dish. Combine the tomato paste, water, and herbs and pour over shells. Sprinkle with remaining mozzarella. Bake, uncovered, for 35 minutes.

Serves 6

Per serving:	Calcium (mg)	Fat (g)	Chol (mg)	Carbo (g)	Protein (g)	Calories
	396	10.6	30	33.1	19.3	300

PASTA PRIMAVERA

1 tablespoon Best Butter (see index)
1 tablespoon arrowroot
1 cup evaporated skim milk
2 tablespoons chopped parsley
1 clove garlic, minced
½ teaspoon salt
Dash cayenne pepper
1 cup green peas, blanched
1 cup broccoli florets, blanched
1 cup sliced mushrooms
1 pound spinach pasta (rotelles, shells, or shape of your choice)
1 cup cherry tomatoes
2 tablespoons grated Parmesan or sapsago cheese
Fresh black pepper to taste

Make Basic White Sauce of first three ingredients (see index). Add chopped parsley, garlic, salt, cayenne, and vegetables, except for tomatoes. Cook, stirring, until mixture just reaches boil and remove from heat. Cook the pasta until tender, about 8 minutes. Drain, toss with cream sauce, tomatoes, and vegetables. Sprinkle on cheese and pepper and toss.

Serves 12

Per ¾-cup serving:	Calcium (mg)	Fat (g)	Chol (mg)	Carbo (g)	Protein (g)	Calories
	62	3.2	39	34.4	7.4	202

MACARONI, TOMATO, AND CHEESE CASSEROLE

8 ounces elbow macaroni (whole wheat preferred)
1 tablespoon Best Butter (see index)
1 tablespoon arrowroot
3 cups skim milk
¾ cup grated part-skim mozzarella cheese
¼ cup grated Romano or sapsago cheese
¼ cup grated cheddar cheese or Formagg
1 teaspoon grated onion
1 teaspoon mustard
½ teaspoon salt
Freshly ground pepper
4 medium tomatoes, peeled and sliced
Chopped fresh parsley

Cook macaroni in boiling water to which a little oil has been added until just tender, about 8 minutes. Drain, run under cold water, and place in mixing bowl. In nonstick skillet, melt Best Butter and blend in arrowroot to form a paste. Add milk and stir until it thickens. Add the cheeses, onion, mustard, salt, and pepper and cook, stirring, until cheese melts. Remove from heat and mix with macaroni. Place half mixture in ovenproof casserole and top with half the tomato slices. Repeat layering then bake in preheated 350°F oven for 20 minutes. Pass under broiler until cheese sauce bubbles. Remove from oven, sprinkle with chopped parsley, and serve.

Serves 8

Per serving:	*Calcium* (mg)	*Fat* (g)	*Chol* (mg)	*Carbo* (g)	*Protein* (g)	*Calories*
	326	7.4	21	25.2	13.4	221

TORTELLINI IN CHEESE SAUCE

2 tablespoons Best Butter (see index)
2 tablespoons arrowroot
2 cups skim milk
2 tablespoons nonfat dry milk
Salt and freshly ground black pepper to taste
1/8 teaspoon freshly grated nutmeg
1/8 teaspoon cayenne pepper
1/4 cup cubed part-skim mozzarella or Swiss cheese
15 ounces fresh cheese-filled tortellini
Vegetable spray
2 tablespoons grated Parmesan cheese

Melt Best Butter in a nonstick saucepan and add arrowroot, stirring to blend. Add the milk and stir with wooden spoon until sauce thickens. Add seasonings and then the cubed cheese. Heat, stirring, until it melts. In the meantime, preheat oven to 450°F and in a large saucepan bring to boil 2 quarts of lightly salted water. Drop tortellini into water and cook until tender, about 5–7 minutes. Drain and turn into vegetable-sprayed baking dish. Spoon cheese sauce over tortellini and sprinkle with Parmesan. Bake for 10 minutes and quickly run under broiler to brown.

Serves 4

Per serving:	*Calcium* (mg)	*Fat* (g)	*Chol* (mg)	*Carbo* (g)	*Protein* (g)	*Calories*
	276	10.5	24	29.6	11.7	262

VEGETABLE PIES

HOT TAMALE PIE

- 1 teaspoon safflower oil
- 1 cup chopped onion
- 1 cup chopped green bell pepper
- ¼ cup chopped celery
- 1¾ cups canned Italian plum tomatoes, crushed
- 1 10-ounce package frozen whole kernel corn
- 2 cups canned red kidney beans, rinsed and drained
- 3 teaspoons (or less) crushed hot red pepper flakes
- 4 cups Vegetable Stock (see index)
- 1½ cups yellow cornmeal
- ½ cup plus 2 tablespoons nonfat dry milk
- Vegetable spray
- ¼ cup shredded sharp cheddar cheese (or Formagg)
- ½ cup shredded part-skim mozzarella cheese

Heat the oil in a large nonstick skillet and cook onion, green pepper, and celery in it until tender. Add tomatoes, corn, kidney beans, and crushed red pepper. Cook, uncovered, for about 15 minutes, until thick, stirring to combine. In another saucepan, heat the Vegetable Stock. Stir in the cornmeal and nonfat dry milk and cook, stirring constantly, until thick and smooth. Remove from heat. Coat a deep 9-inch square baking pan (or 2 smaller casseroles) with vegetable spray. Pour in the cornmeal mixture, then the bean and tomato sauce. Combine the shredded cheeses and sprinkle on top of the pie. Bake in preheated 350°F oven for 40–45 minutes, until bubbly.

Serves 6–8

Per serving:	Calcium (mg)	Fat (g)	Chol (mg)	Carbo (g)	Protein (g)	Calories
	171	4.2	9	43.5	12.5	256

NICE RICE PIE

1 teaspoon vegetable oil
6 ounces fresh mushrooms, sliced
Vegetable spray
1 cup Basic Brown Rice (see index)
2 eggs (1 yolk only), beaten
½ cup low-fat cottage cheese
½ cup part-skim ricotta cheese
¼ cup grated Parmesan or sapsago cheese
½ cup grated part-skim mozzarella cheese (or any low-fat mild cheese)
1 cup Swiss chard, spinach, kale, or a combination, steamed and chopped

Heat vegetable oil in nonstick skillet and sauté mushrooms in it. Drain. Coat an 8-inch pie pan with vegetable spray and press cooked rice into pan to form crust. Mix the remaining ingredients together to blend and spoon over the rice. Bake, uncovered, in preheated 350°F oven for 15 minutes.

Serves 6

Per serving:	Calcium (mg)	Fat (g)	Chol (mg)	Carbo (g)	Protein (g)	Calories
	257	7.6	66	10.2	13.4	164

BROCCOLI RICOTTA PIE

2 cups part-skim ricotta cheese
2 eggs, beaten
1 cup chopped broccoli florets and some stems
6 leaves spinach or chard, well washed
¼ cup finely chopped onion
2 tablespoons chopped fresh basil *or* 1 teaspoon crumbled dried basil
1 tablespoon whole wheat flour
1 tablespoon all-purpose unbleached flour
½ cup grated part-skim mozzarella cheese
Cayenne, nutmeg, and freshly ground pepper to taste
1 unbaked Perfect Pie Crust (see index)
Paprika

Mix all ingredients except crust and paprika together. Turn into the unbaked pie shell and sprinkle with paprika. Bake in preheated 375°F oven for 40–45 minutes.

Serves 8

Per serving:	*Calcium* (mg)	*Fat* (g)	*Chol* (mg)	*Carbo* (g)	*Protein* (g)	*Calories*
	273	13.5	94	18.2	15.0	250

MEATLESS MOUSSAKA

1 medium eggplant
Salt
1 tablespoon vegetable oil
1 cup chopped onion
2 cloves garlic, minced
8 ounces mushrooms, sliced
¼ cup chopped fresh parsley
2 stalks celery, chopped
1 cup canned Italian plum tomatoes
½ cup dry red wine
1 teaspoon dried mint, crumbled
¼ teaspoon ground cinnamon
½ teaspoon dried thyme
Salt and freshly ground pepper to taste
1 cup part-skim ricotta cheese
1 egg
¼ cup grated Parmesan or sapsago cheese
1 teaspoon dried basil
Vegetable oil

Preheat oven to 350°F. Peel and slice the eggplant. Sprinkle lightly with salt and drain. Heat oil in a skillet and brown the onion and garlic in it. Add mushrooms, parsley, celery, tomatoes, wine, mint, cinnamon, thyme, and salt and pepper. Simmer until liquid is absorbed. In a separate bowl, mix together the ricotta, egg, half the Parmesan, and the basil. Coat a casserole with vegetable oil and layer in it half the eggplant, half the tomato mixture, and half the cheese. Repeat layers and top with remaining Parmesan. Bake, uncovered, for 45 minutes.

Serves 6

Per serving:	*Calcium* (mg)	*Fat* (g)	*Chol* (mg)	*Carbo* (g)	*Protein* (g)	*Calories*
	198	7.7	19.8	13.4	9.5	171

FANTASTIC FRITTATA

3-4 medium-size leeks, well washed and trimmed
1 cup chopped Swiss chard
1 cup tofu (bean curd)
½ cup low-fat cottage cheese
¾ cup skim milk
2 tablespoons arrowroot
½ teaspoon low-sodium soy sauce
Salt and freshly ground pepper to taste
3 tablespoons grated Parmesan or sapsago cheese
Paprika

Preheat oven to 350°F. Slice cleaned leeks into ¼-inch rings. Steam leeks and chard. Drain. Set aside. Combine remaining ingredients except the Parmesan and paprika in a food processor and blend until smooth. Place vegetables in a 9-inch pie pan and pour tofu mixture over them. Sprinkle with grated cheese and a dash of paprika for color. Bake, uncovered, for 20–30 minutes, until nicely browned.

Serves 6

	Calcium (mg)	Fat (g)	Chol (mg)	Carbo (g)	Protein (g)	Calories
Per serving:	187	3.5	3.3	9.2	10	105

TOFU PARMESAN

2 cakes firm tofu (bean curd) (2 cups)
1 teaspoon vegetable oil
1 cup chopped onion
1 cup chopped green bell pepper
10 ounces tomato sauce
1 cup chopped mushrooms
Dash cayenne pepper
Vegetable spray
3 tablespoons chopped fresh oregano *or* 2 teaspoons dried, crumbled
6 ounces part-skim mozzarella cheese, cut into thin slices
2 tablespoons grated Parmesan or sapsago cheese
1 tablespoon wheat germ

Cut tofu into ½-inch slices and press in paper toweling to remove excess moisture. Heat oil in a nonstick skillet and sauté onion in it. Add green pepper, tomato sauce, and mushrooms and bring to simmer. Cook over low heat for 20 minutes. Add cayenne and stir. Place half the tofu slices in a layer in a vegetable-sprayed 8-inch baking dish, then layer half the oregano, mozzarella, tomato sauce, and grated cheese. Repeat layering until all ingredients are used up. Sprinkle on the wheat germ and bake, covered with foil, in a 350°F oven for 30 minutes or until cheese is melted.

Serves 6

Per serving:	*Calcium* (mg)	*Fat* (g)	*Chol* (mg)	*Carbo* (g)	*Protein* (g)	*Calories*
	323	13.6	17	11.1	15.8	222

BREAKFAST AND BRUNCH FARE

APPLE PANCAKES

½ cup part-skim ricotta cheese
½ cup low-fat cottage cheese
1 cup grated peeled apple, packed tight
1 tablespoon concentrated frozen orange juice
1 teaspoon fresh lemon juice
2 tablespoons chopped dried figs
¼ cup chopped almonds and hazelnuts
Dash freshly grated nutmeg
Dash ground cinnamon
2 eggs (1 yolk only), beaten
¾ cup whole wheat flour
Vegetable spray

Mix together all ingredients except flour and vegetable spray. Gradually stir in whole wheat flour. Lightly spray a nonstick griddle and heat until a drop of water bounces off it. Use about ¼ cup of batter for each pancake. Spoon onto griddle and cook until bubbles form, then flip and flatten out and brown on other side. Keep warm. Serve with extra dollop of yogurt and fresh fruit, Saucy Orange Chiffon (see index), or any other creamy topping.

Yields 12 pancakes

Per serving (3 pancakes without toppings):	*Calcium* (mg)	*Fat* (g)	*Chol* (mg)	*Carbo* (g)	*Protein* (g)	*Calories*
	153	9.5	79	34.9	4.1	269

PUFFY PANCAKES

1 cup low-fat cottage cheese
1 egg yolk
2 tablespoons nonfat dry milk
1 tablespoon concentrated frozen orange juice
½ teaspoon baking powder
½ cup whole wheat flour
Vegetable spray
2 egg whites, beaten until stiff
1 tablespoon sunflower seeds or sesame seeds
½ cup orange-flavored Yogurt Sour Cream (see note below)
Berries (optional)

In a blender, mix together cottage cheese, egg yolk, dry milk, orange juice concentrate, baking powder, and flour. Add a bit of water to thin batter. Coat a nonstick skillet with vegetable spray and heat until a drop of water bounces when sprinkled on pan. In the meantime, fold beaten egg whites into batter and use 2 tablespoons of batter to form each pancake (use 1 tablespoon if smaller pancakes are preferred). When bubbles form on top of the pancakes, sprinkle a few sunflower or sesame seeds on each and flip over to brown on the other side. Top with Yogurt Sour Cream and berries, if desired, or use yogurt mixed with sugar-free conserve.

Note: To make ½ cup orange-flavored Yogurt Sour Cream, follow recipe for Yogurt Sour Cream (see index), using 1 cup plain nonfat or low-fat yogurt and 1 tablespoon concentrated frozen orange juice.

Serves 4

Per 3-pancake serving:	*Calcium* (mg)	*Fat* (g)	*Chol* (mg)	*Carbo* (g)	*Protein* (g)	*Calories*
	193	4.2	74	23	15.9	192

BEAUTIFUL BLINTZES

Crepes

1 tablespoon (more if needed) Best Butter (see index)
1 egg
1½ cups buttermilk
½ cup plain low-fat yogurt
½ cup unbleached all-purpose flour
½ cup whole wheat flour

Heat a nonstick griddle pan and coat with some Best Butter. Mix remaining ingredients until smooth and pour about ¼ cup batter onto griddle, tilting to spread batter thinly. Cook quickly over high heat, turning until lightly browned on each side. Repeat to make 12 crepes. (To freeze, place crepes between sheets of plastic wrap; defrost before proceeding with recipe.) If not freezing crepes, stack carefully or arrange on platter before filling.

Makes 12 crepes

Per 1-crepe serving:	*Calcium* (mg)	*Fat* (g)	*Chol* (mg)	*Carbo* (g)	*Protein* (g)	*Calories*
	58	2.1	26	9.4	3.2	68

Cheese Filling

Vegetable spray
2 cups low-fat cottage cheese
1 teaspoon pure vanilla extract
1 teaspoon ground cinnamon
¼ cup raisins
12 crepes

Coat a baking dish with vegetable spray. Preheat oven to 375°F. Combine all ingredients and spoon about 2 tablespoons on each crepe. Fold sides and edges together to make tight bundle. Place side by side in baking dish and bake for 20 minutes. Sprinkle tops with additional cinnamon. If desired, top with dab of Great Grape Jelly or Saucy Orange Chiffon Sauce (see index).

Makes 12 blintzes

Per serving (filled blintz without topping):	*Calcium* (mg)	*Fat* (g)	*Chol* (mg)	*Carbo* (g)	*Protein* (g)	*Calories*
	83	2.5	28	13.2	8.0	106

Apple Filling

Vegetable spray
2 cups finely chopped peeled apples
1 tablespoon arrowroot
¼ cup orange juice
½ teaspoon ground cinnamon
¼ cup plain low-fat yogurt
1 teaspoon concentrated frozen orange juice
8 crepes
1 tablespoon grated orange zest

Preheat oven to 375°F and coat baking dish with vegetable spray. Combine apples, arrowroot, orange juice, and cinnamon and cook in a saucepan until the apples are just soft. Combine the yogurt and orange juice concentrate and reserve. Spoon about 2 tablespoons of the apple mixture onto each crepe and fold the edges together to seal. Place them in baking dish side by side and bake for about 20 minutes. Serve with a dollop of orange yogurt garnished with sprinkling of orange zest.

Makes 8 blintzes

Per serving (filled blintz):	*Calcium* (mg)	*Fat* (g)	*Chol* (mg)	*Carbo* (g)	*Protein* (g)	*Calories*
	75	2.4	26	18.4	8	106

Blueberry-Cheese Filling

Vegetable spray
1½ cup fresh blueberries, picked over and rinsed
1 tablespoon arrowroot
2 teaspoons crystalline fructose
½ cup low-fat cottage cheese
½ cup part-skim ricotta cheese
½ teaspoon ground cinnamon
8 crepes

Preheat oven to 375°F and coat a baking dish with vegetable spray. Combine 1 cup of blueberries, arrowroot, and fructose in a saucepan and cook until slightly thickened. Mix together the cottage cheese, ricotta, and cinnamon. Place 1 tablespoon of the cheese mixture and 1 tablespoon of the blueberry sauce on each crepe. Seal the edges tightly and place blintzes side by side in baking dish. Bake about 20 minutes. Garnish with the remaining berries.

Makes 8 blintzes

Per serving (filled blintz):	*Calcium* (mg)	*Fat* (g)	*Chol* (mg)	*Carbo* (g)	*Protein* (g)	*Calories*
	110	3.6	31	15.8	6.9	120

FRENCH TOAST TREAT

2 egg whites
½ cup skim milk
2 tablespoons nonfat dry milk
½ teaspoon pure vanilla extract
1 teaspoon concentrated frozen orange juice
Ground cinnamon to taste
4 slices whole wheat bread
1 teaspoon Best Butter (see index)

Beat the egg whites until frothy. Add the milks, vanilla, orange juice, and cinnamon. Dip the bread slices into this and coat well. In a nonstick skillet or griddle, melt the Best Butter and brown the bread. Top with Great Grape Jelly (see index) or other sugar-free conserve.

Serves 4

Per serving:	*Calcium* (mg)	*Fat* (g)	*Chol* (mg)	*Carbo* (g)	*Protein* (g)	*Calories*
	88	1.8	3.1	14.2	5.8	93

WONDERFUL WAFFLES

1 egg
1 cup whole wheat flour
2 tablespoons cornmeal
2 teaspoons crystalline fructose
¼ cup nonfat dry milk
1 cup buttermilk
2 tablespoons safflower oil
2 teaspoons baking powder

Place all ingredients in blender and process until smooth. Turn into waffle iron and cook according to instructions, removing when brown. Serve with fresh fruit and yogurt or kefir, or with sherbet, or with Crème Fraîche, Whipped Ricotta Cream, or a dessert sauce (see index).

Makes 4 double waffles or 4 servings

Per serving:	Calcium (mg)	Fat (g)	Chol (mg)	Carbo (g)	Protein (g)	Calories
	178	9.4	72	31.4	9.4	241

BUTTERMILK BLUEBERRY BAKE

⅓ cup whole wheat flour
⅓ cup all-purpose flour
2 teaspoons baking powder
2 tablespoons concentrated frozen orange juice
1 tablespoon crystalline fructose
1 cup buttermilk
Vegetable spray
2 cups fresh blueberries, picked over and rinsed
Orange-flavored Yogurt Sour Cream (see index) or part-skim ricotta (optional)

Mix together the flours, baking powder, orange juice concentrate, and fructose and gradually add buttermilk, stirring until blended. Coat an 8-inch baking dish with vegetable spray and pour in batter. Top with blueberries and place in preheated 350°F oven until puffy and lightly browned, about 40–45 minutes. Top with Yogurt Sour Cream or ricotta, if desired.

Serves 6

Per serving:	Calcium (mg)	Fat (g)	Chol (mg)	Carbo (g)	Protein (g)	Calories
	79	.8	2	21.4	3.2	101

OATMEAL SOUFFLE

3 cups skim milk, divided
1 cup rolled oats
1 teaspoon baking powder
½ teaspoon salt
½ tablespoon crystalline fructose
2 tablespoons walnut oil
3 eggs (only 1½ yolks), separated
Vegetable spray
1 tablespoon sunflower seeds
Ground cinnamon

Pour 2 cups of the skim milk into a saucepan and heat to the boil. Then add the oats and simmer until thickened, stirring. Remove from heat and add the baking powder, salt, fructose, walnut oil, and remaining cup of milk. Beat the egg yolks into the oatmeal. In the meantime, beat egg whites until they stand in peaks. Fold into oatmeal mixture. Coat a 1-quart soufflé dish with vegetable spray and preheat oven to 350°F. Turn combined batter into the baking dish, sprinkle sunflower seeds on top, and bake for 30–35 minutes, until puffy and lightly browned. Sprinkle with cinnamon and serve. Nice served for breakfast, brunch, or lunch with fresh fruit.

Serves 4

Per serving:	*Calcium* (mg)	*Fat* (g)	*Chol* (mg)	*Carbo* (g)	*Protein* (g)	*Calories*
	273	11.9	106	30	14.9	286

CHEESE AND TOFU SOUFFLE

Vegetable spray
3 slices whole wheat bread, halved
6 ounces firm tofu (bean curd), cut into ½-inch-thick slices
4 ounces grated part-skim mozzarella cheese
1½ cups skim milk
2 egg whites, beaten
2 tablespoons red miso (see Chapter 12)
1 teaspoon chopped jalapeño pepper
½ teaspoon celery salt
¼ teaspoon onion powder
1 teaspoon toasted sesame seeds
4 cherry tomatoes, halved

Lightly coat a 1-quart casserole with vegetable spray and make layers of the bread, tofu slices, and cheese, repeating until all ingredients are used. Combine in a separate bowl the milk, egg whites, miso, pepper, celery salt, and onion powder. Pour into casserole and let stand 1–2 hours. Sprinkle top with sesame seeds and place the tomatoes around the bread and tofu pieces. Preheat oven to 350°F and put casserole in a pan of boiling water. Place both in the oven and bake for about an hour or until sides of the soufflé separate from the bowl and top is browned. Remove from oven and serve at once with a salad and fruit, if desired.

Serves 4

Per serving:	*Calcium* (mg)	*Fat* (g)	*Chol* (mg)	*Carbo* (g)	*Protein* (g)	*Calories*
	376	27.4	18	15.6	17.4	193

COTTAGE CHEESE SOUFFLE

1 cup low-fat cottage cheese
2 tablespoons grated Parmesan or sapsago cheese
2 eggs (1 yolk only), separated
½ teaspoon arrowroot
2 tablespoons evaporated skim milk
¼ teaspoon dried dill weed
¼ teaspoon salt
Dash white pepper
Vegetable spray
Paprika

Preheat oven to 350°F. Combine cottage cheese, Parmesan or sapsago (reserve 1 teaspoon), egg yolk, arrowroot, milk, dill weed, and salt and pepper. Beat egg whites until they form stiff peaks. Fold gently into cottage cheese mixture only until blended. Spoon into vegetable-sprayed soufflé dish. Sprinkle remaining Parmesan or sapsago and paprika on top. Bake for 20–25 minutes, until soufflé is puffy and nicely browned. Serve immediately upon removing from oven. Nice with a leafy green salad and toasted bread.

Serves 2

Per serving:	*Calcium* (mg)	*Fat* (g)	*Chol* (mg)	*Carbo* (g)	*Protein* (g)	*Calories*
	172	5.5	146	7.7	22	174

4
VEGETABLES

Mother was on the right track when she said, "Eat your spinach," but she would have been better advised to suggest broccoli, kale, or collards. These green vegetables provide calcium that is more readily absorbed by the body. Okra and turnip tops are also good calcium sources. Many vegetables, such as mustard greens, spinach, Swiss chard, beet tops, parsley, and chives, are bound with oxalic acids that often prevent maximum calcium absorption by the digestive system. Some say that cooking will free up the calcium. Small quantities of these greens are certainly recommended. Most are interchangeable: recipes calling for spinach may be made with chard or turnip tops or cabbage. Collards may be cooked with sunflower seeds, nutmeg, cardamom, and other spices. Stir-fried vegetables with various seasonings, sesame seeds, or the addition of soy nuts are healthful and easy to prepare. "Cream" sauce is a high-calcium boost for many fresh vegetables. Additional garnishes of bell pepper, shredded cheese, and wheat germ add color and texture.

Select only produce that is brightly colored and unwilted. Fresh vegetables are recommended and have more nutrients than frozen foods. The leafy greens need to be washed carefully: dipped several times in tepid water in the sink and run under cold water. Steam them with just the water remaining on the washed leaves. Discolored leaves and tough stems should be discarded before cooking.

Vegetables may be baked or sautéed in a little oil or Best Butter (see index), but the best method of cooking to preserve the nutrients is steaming or blanching quickly in boiling water and then draining and running under cold water or plunging into ice water. Do not add baking soda when cooking vegetables. Save the cooking water to make vegetable stock.

Many vegetables may be used raw in salads, and they too can be enhanced by garnishes such as sesame seeds, pimientos, red peppers, shredded carrots, mushrooms, and bean sprouts.

ARTICHOKES

4 globe artichokes
Juice of ½ lemon
1 tablespoon vinegar

Cut stems off the artichokes and trim off small leaves at base. Trim about ½ inch off tops and cut points off remaining leaves. Rinse in cold water and rub with lemon juice. Immerse chokes in vinegar and water until ready to cook. In the meantime, bring to boil 4 quarts of water with some salt. Place artichokes in pot, cover with 2 layers of cheesecloth, and boil, uncovered, for 30–40 minutes, until leaves pull off easily. Drain upside down in a colander. Serve warm or cold with Balsamic Vinaigrette or Lemon Sauce (see index for recipes).

Serves 4

Per serving (without sauce):	*Calcium* (mg)	*Fat* (g)	*Chol* (mg)	*Carbo* (g)	*Protein* (g)	*Calories*
	63	.2	0	13	3.5	35

ASPARAGUS AND PIMIENTO

1 pound fresh asparagus or broccoli
½ cup cold water
1 large pimiento, rinsed and cut into julienne strips
2 tablespoons fresh lime juice
1 tablespoon sesame seeds, toasted

Rinse asparagus and snap off tough ends. (If using broccoli, cut into florets.) Bring water to boil in a large skillet and add asparagus or broccoli. Cover and steam until just tender, about 3–4 minutes. Remove from heat, drain, and run under cold water. Arrange on serving platter, decorate with pimiento strips, and sprinkle with lime juice and sesame seeds. Serve warm or chilled.

Serves 4

Per serving (using asparagus):	*Calcium* (mg)	*Fat* (g)	*Chol* (mg)	*Carbo* (g)	*Protein* (g)	*Calories*
	31	1.1	0	5.5	3.3	41

Per serving (using broccoli):	*Calcium* (mg)	*Fat* (g)	*Chol* (mg)	*Carbo* (g)	*Protein* (g)	*Calories*
	130	1.8	0	8	5.4	57

BOK CHOY

1 pound bok choy (Chinese celery)
1 tablespoon corn oil
½ teaspoon minced garlic
½ teaspoon crystalline fructose
1 teaspoon low-sodium soy sauce
Few drops sesame oil

Rinse bok choy in cold water. Cut stalks into 1-inch pieces and the leaves into thin shreds. Heat oil in a large nonstick skillet. Add the stems first and sauté, tossing, about 2 minutes. Then add the garlic, leaves, fructose, soy sauce, and sesame oil and continue cooking over high heat for another 2 minutes. This is also nice served with cooked bean sprouts or mixed with other vegetables.

Serves 4

Per serving:	*Calcium* (mg)	*Fat* (g)	*Chol* (mg)	*Carbo* (g)	*Protein* (g)	*Calories*
	64	3.7	0	7.1	1.8	63

MUSTARD BROCCOLI AND CAULIFLOWER

2 cups fresh broccoli florets
2 cups fresh cauliflower florets
Vegetable spray
1 tablespoon Best Butter (see index)
1 tablespoon arrowroot
1 cup skim milk
2 teaspoons Dijon mustard
Dash onion powder
Freshly ground pepper to taste
2 tablespoons grated sharp cheddar cheese (or Formagg)
Paprika

Blanch the broccoli and cauliflower pieces and drain. Place in vegetable-sprayed ovenproof dish. In the meantime, melt Best Butter in nonstick skillet, mix with arrowroot until smooth, then add the milk, mustard, onion powder, and pepper. Stir until sauce becomes thick, then add the cheese and continue stirring until it melts. Spoon sauce over the vegetables, sprinkle with a little paprika and cook for 15–20 minutes in preheated 350°F oven, then run quickly under broiler to brown.

Serves 4

Per serving:	*Calcium* (mg)	*Fat* (g)	*Chol* (mg)	*Carbo* (g)	*Protein* (g)	*Calories*
	159	4.9	9	12.4	7.6	114

SESAME BROCCOLI

1 pound fresh broccoli, trimmed and cut into florets
1 tablespoon toasted sesame seeds
1 teaspoon sesame oil
1 tablespoon rice wine vinegar
¼ teaspoon hot red pepper flakes
Juice of ½ lemon

Steam broccoli florets over boiling water until tender, about 2–3 minutes. Transfer to serving bowl. (Save the pot water for Vegetable Stock [see index for recipe].) Combine remaining ingredients and drizzle over warm broccoli.

Serves 4

Per serving:	*Calcium* (mg)	*Fat* (g)	*Chol* (mg)	*Carbo* (g)	*Protein* (g)	*Calories*
	120	3	0	11.1	6.9	82

ONION CREAMED BRUSSELS SPROUTS

1 pound brussels sprouts, trimmed and rinsed
¼ cup chopped onion
1 clove garlic, chopped fine
1 teaspoon safflower oil
½ cup plain low-fat yogurt
2 tablespoons nonfat dry milk
1 tablespoon chopped fresh dill *or* 1 teaspoon dried, crumbled

Drop sprouts into boiling water and cook until tender, about 10 minutes. In the meantime, in nonstick skillet sauté the onion and garlic in heated oil. When sprouts are cooked, drain and mix together with the onions and add yogurt and milk to the skillet. Remove from heat for this step to prevent yogurt from separating. Sprinkle with fresh or dried dill and serve.

Serves 4

Per serving:	Calcium (mg)	Fat (g)	Chol (mg)	Carbo (g)	Protein (g)	Calories
	104	1.8	2	11.7	6.2	78

CABBAGE 'N' SPROUTS

1 tablespoon vegetable oil
1 cup sliced onion
1 cup Chicken Stock (see index)
1 teaspoon salt
1 teaspoon celery salt
3 cups shredded green cabbage (about ¾ pound)
1½ cups bean sprouts, rinsed

In nonstick skillet, heat oil and sauté onion in it about 3 minutes. Add the Chicken Stock, salt, and celery salt, mixing well. Then add the cabbage and cook, covered, about 5 minutes. Add sprouts, stir, and cook another 3 minutes, until cabbage is tender but still crisp.

Serves 4

Per serving:	Calcium (mg)	Fat (g)	Chol (mg)	Carbo (g)	Protein (g)	Calories
	43	3.8	0	8.5	3	73

SPICY YOGURT CABBAGE

½ cup minced onion
1 small red cabbage, rough leaves removed, rinsed, and shredded (about 3 cups)
1½ cups peeled and chopped apples
¼ teaspoon curry powder
⅛ teaspoon ground allspice
1 teaspoon salt
1 cup plain low-fat or nonfat yogurt

Heat a large nonstick skillet and add the onion and shredded cabbage, cooking until it wilts. Add the apples, spices, and salt and cook another 20 minutes, until the apples are soft. Remove from heat and rapidly stir in yogurt.

Serves 4

Per serving:	*Calcium* (mg)	*Fat* (g)	*Chol* (mg)	*Carbo* (g)	*Protein* (g)	*Calories*
	138	1.2	4	16.4	4	86

HOT COLLARDS

1 pound collard greens or mustard greens, turnip greens, or kale
2 cups Chicken Stock or Vegetable Stock (see index)
1 cup fresh chard leaves
3–4 leaves fresh basil
1 tablespoon walnut oil
¾ cup chopped onion
2 cloves garlic, minced
1 tablespoon grated fresh ginger
1 jalapeño pepper, stem and seeds discarded, minced
2 dashes sesame oil
Salt and freshly ground black pepper to taste
1 teaspoon sesame seeds

Wash greens well, dipping into tepid water several times, and slice into thin strips. Place in nonstick pot with the broth, chard, and basil and cook, covered, for about 30 minutes, until greens are tender. In another large nonstick skillet, heat oil and soften onion and garlic in it. Add ginger and jalapeño and stir together. Add collards and stir until liquid is nearly evaporated. Add sesame oil and salt and pepper to taste and stir. When serving, garnish with sprinkling of sesame seeds.

Serves 4

Per serving:	*Calcium* (mg)	*Fat* (g)	*Chol* (mg)	*Carbo* (g)	*Protein* (g)	*Calories*
	184	6.1	1	9.8	5.6	103

DILLED GREEN BEANS

1 teaspoon safflower oil
2 cloves garlic, minced
1½ tablespoons wheat germ
1 tablespoon chopped scallion
1 tablespoon chopped fresh dill *or* 1 teaspoon dried
1 pound green beans, trimmed (about 3 cups)
3 tablespoons chopped fresh parsley

In nonstick skillet, heat oil and in it brown garlic, wheat germ, scallion, and dill. In another saucepan, bring to boil 2 cups water. Drop beans in and cook about 3–4 minutes. Drain and run under cold water to stop cooking. Serve warm, topped with dill mixture and parsley.

Serves 4

Per serving:	*Calcium* (mg)	*Fat* (g)	*Chol* (mg)	*Carbo* (g)	*Protein* (g)	*Calories*
	51	1.4	0	7.7	2.4	46

GREEN BEANS AMANDINE

1 clove garlic, chopped
2 tablespoons blanched almonds
½ cup sliced scallions
¼ cup minced fresh parsley
¼ cup fresh lemon juice
Dash cayenne pepper
1 teaspoon Dijon mustard
½ cup plain low-fat yogurt
1 pound fresh green beans, trimmed and washed

In a blender, grind the garlic and almonds, then add remaining ingredients except the yogurt and beans. Remove nut mixture from blender and stir into the yogurt. Steam or blanch the beans until just tender, about 5 minutes, then drain. Mix the sauce with the beans in a warm saucepan but do not cook further.

Serves 4

Per serving:	*Calcium* (mg)	*Fat* (g)	*Chol* (mg)	*Carbo* (g)	*Protein* (g)	*Calories*
	123	2.8	2	11.8	4.5	82

QUICK BRAISED KALE

3 pounds fresh kale
1 tablespoon corn oil
½ cup chopped onion
1 clove garlic, minced
1 teaspoon salt
¼ teaspoon freshly ground pepper
3 tablespoons water
2 teaspoons fresh lemon juice
1 teaspoon Durkee's Imitation Bacon Bits

Wash the kale several times and remove tough stems. Chop fine. Heat oil in nonstick skillet and sauté onion and garlic in it until brown. Then add remaining ingredients except lemon juice and Bacon Bits. Cook over medium heat for 15–20 minutes, until tender, and then stir in lemon juice and Bacon Bits. Adjust seasoning and serve.

Serves 6

Per serving:	*Calcium* (mg)	*Fat* (g)	*Chol* (mg)	*Carbo* (g)	*Protein* (g)	*Calories*
	211	3.3	0	8.2	6	75

HUNGARIAN KOHLRABI

1 tablespoon Best Butter (see index)
1 pound kohlrabi (about 6 knobs), peeled and diced
½ teaspoon crystalline fructose
4 tablespoons chopped fresh parsley
½ cup Chicken Stock (see index)

Heat Best Butter in a nonstick skillet and add the remaining ingredients. Cook, covered, for about 30 minutes, until kohlrabi is tender.

Serves 4

Per serving:	*Calcium* (mg)	*Fat* (g)	*Chol* (mg)	*Carbo* (g)	*Protein* (g)	*Calories*
	50	3.4	4	7.6	2.4	64

LEEKS VINAIGRETTE

8 medium leeks, trimmed and well washed
Balsamic Vinaigrette (see index)

Split the trimmed leeks lengthwise, leaving the white root ends whole. Make certain all sand is rinsed away. Bundle the leeks and tie with string. Drop into a saucepan of boiling salted water and simmer, covered, for about 12 minutes, until just tender. Serve immediately with 1 tablespoon of vinaigrette or place in ice water to stop cooking. Save and freeze the cooking liquid for use in Vegetable Stock (see index for recipe).

Serves 4

Per serving:	*Calcium* (mg)	*Fat* (g)	*Chol* (mg)	*Carbo* (g)	*Protein* (g)	*Calories*
	106	20	1	18.5	2.6	97

LADY RAINBOW OKRA

5 cups tender small okra pods (about 1 pound)
2 egg whites, beaten
1 cup cornmeal
1 tablespoon cayenne pepper
1 tablespoon vegetable oil (or a little more as needed)

Trim ends of okra and cut into ¼-inch slices. Toss pods in egg white to coat. Mix cornmeal and cayenne in a paper bag, drop okra into the bag in small quantities, and shake to coat. Heat oil in a large nonstick skillet and gradually add okra, cooking quickly over high heat until browned.

Serves 6

Per serving:	*Calcium* (mg)	*Fat* (g)	*Chol* (mg)	*Carbo* (g)	*Protein* (g)	*Calories*
	100	2.8	0	15.5	4.2	97

MARINATED OKRA PODS

1 pound fresh small okra pods, trimmed
¼ cup red wine vinegar
¼ teaspoon salt
2 tablespoons virgin olive oil
1 small red onion, sliced into rings
2 tablespoons fresh lemon juice
Romaine lettuce leaves
2 cups cherry tomatoes

Blanch trimmed okra in boiling water for a minute or two and then drain and plunge into ice water to stop cooking. Drain once again and pat dry. In the meantime, mix the remaining ingredients except the lettuce and tomatoes. Pour the marinade into a glass container, add the okra, cover, and refrigerate for a few hours. When ready to serve, drain and place on bed of lettuce with the cherry tomatoes. Top with some of the onion rings, drained.

Serves 6

Per serving:	*Calcium* (mg)	*Fat* (g)	*Chol* (mg)	*Carbo* (g)	*Protein* (g)	*Calories*
	107	4.9	0	10.7	3	89

OKRA

1 pound small fresh okra pods

Trim off okra stems and points and rinse under cold water. Drop into pot of boiling water and blanch for 2 minutes. Drain and run under cold water or drop into bowl of ice water to stop cooking. Place on paper toweling to dry. These are now ready to eat, or they may be set aside for use in other dishes; added to salads, to tomato sauces, or stews; or run quickly under broiler to reheat.

Serves 4

Per serving:	*Calcium* (mg)	*Fat* (g)	*Chol* (mg)	*Carbo* (g)	*Protein* (g)	*Calories*
	110	.4	0	7.2	24	35

OKRA PROVENÇAL

1 pound small fresh okra pods, trimmed
12 ounces canned Italian plum tomatoes
4 scallions, chopped
2 cloves garlic, minced
½ cup chopped green pepper
8 small pimiento-stuffed olives
4 tablespoons chopped fresh parsley
Pinch each dried thyme and dried marjoram
2 tablespoons chopped fresh basil *or* 2 teaspoons dried, crumbled
Salt and freshly ground black pepper to taste

Blanch the trimmed okra pods in boiling water for a minute. Drain and run quickly under cold water. Set aside on paper towel until ready to use. In the meantime, place remaining ingredients in a large saucepan and simmer until sauce becomes thick, about 30 minutes. Adjust seasoning. Turn okra into the sauce, stir, and cook until just tender, but not so long that the okra becomes mushy.

Serves 4

Per serving:	*Calcium* (mg)	*Fat* (g)	*Chol* (mg)	*Carbo* (g)	*Protein* (g)	*Calories*
	141	1.6	0	14.7	4.3	79

PARSNIP PUREE

6 medium parsnips (about 2 cups), peeled and trimmed
2 tablespoons plain lowfat yogurt
2 tablespoons nonfat dry milk
¼ teaspoon ground mace
¼ teaspoon freshly grated nutmeg

Cook parsnips in boiling salt water until tender, about 20 minutes. Drain and place in blender or processor to puree, along with the yogurt and milk. Add the spices and more yogurt if consistency needs adjusting.

Serves 4

Per serving:	*Calcium* (mg)	*Fat* (g)	*Chol* (mg)	*Carbo* (g)	*Protein* (g)	*Calories*
	79	.6	1	15.2	2.4	73

PARIS GREEN PEAS

2 cups shelled fresh green peas (about 1½ pounds in pods) *or* lima beans
1 tablespoon minced onion
1 tablespoon Best Butter (see index)
1 cup boiling water
½ teaspoon salt
¼ teaspoon crystalline fructose
2 cups shredded chicory (¼ pound) *or* leaf lettuce
1 teaspoon dried mint

Wash the peas (or lima beans) and combine in saucepan with onion, Best Butter, and boiling water. Cover tightly and simmer for 5–10 minutes. Add salt, fructose, and shredded chicory. Stir, cover, and cook another 2 minutes. Add mint, stir, and serve at once.

Serves 4

Per serving (using peas):	*Calcium* (mg)	*Fat* (g)	*Chol* (mg)	*Carbo* (g)	*Protein* (g)	*Calories*
	22	3.4	4	9.8	4.1	83

Per serving (using lima beans):	*Calcium* (mg)	*Fat* (g)	*Chol* (mg)	*Carbo* (g)	*Protein* (g)	*Calories*
	36	3.3	4	19.1	6.3	128

RUTABAGA PUREE

1 rutabaga (about 1 pound), peeled and diced
1 medium potato, peeled and diced
¼ teaspoon cayenne pepper
½ teaspoon freshly grated nutmeg
4 tablespoons nonfat dry milk
3 tablespoons chopped fresh parsley

Place rutabaga and potato pieces in a saucepan and cover with water. Bring to boil and simmer, covered, for 30 minutes, or until vegetables are tender. Reserve some of the water in case the puree needs thinning. Drain and place in a food processor and puree. Add cayenne, nutmeg, and milk and blend. Rewarm in saucepan before serving with a garnish of chopped parsley. This is particularly healthful and colorful if served inside a ring of steamed broccoli florets.

Serves 6

Per serving:	*Calcium* (mg)	*Fat* (g)	*Chol* (mg)	*Carbo* (g)	*Protein* (g)	*Calories*
	90	.2	1	11.6	2.2	55

CREAMED SPINACH AND MUSHROOMS

2 pounds fresh spinach, well washed, tough stems trimmed
1 tablespoon Best Butter (see index)
½ cup trimmed and chopped fresh mushrooms
1 tablespoon minced onion
½ cup evaporated skim milk
½ teaspoon salt
⅛ teaspoon freshly ground pepper
Dash freshly grated nutmeg

Place the still wet spinach leaves in a large saucepan and cook over high heat, stirring, until spinach is wilted. Heat Best Butter in a nonstick skillet, add mushroom pieces and onion, and cook about 5 minutes. Add remaining ingredients and heat, stirring. In the meantime, drain the spinach well and chop. Combine with the mushroom sauce and serve.

Serves 4

Per serving:	*Calcium* (mg)	*Fat* (g)	*Chol* (mg)	*Carbo* (g)	*Protein* (g)	*Calories*
	213	3.6	4	8	6.0	78

SPINACH

1 teaspoon safflower oil
2 cloves garlic, minced
2 pounds fresh spinach (cooks down to 2 cups)
4 dashes sesame oil
2 teaspoons sesame seeds, toasted

In nonstick skillet, heat safflower oil and sauté garlic in it. Remove from pan and reserve. Wash spinach well, shake off excess moisture, and add to skillet. Cook until wilted, about 5 minutes. Drain off water and toss with garlic and sesame oil. Serve warm or chilled, sprinkled with sesame seeds.

Serves 4

Per serving:	*Calcium* (mg)	*Fat* (g)	*Chol* (mg)	*Carbo* (g)	*Protein* (g)	*Calories*
	118	2.7	0	4.4	3.6	48

SQUASH AND PEPPER SALAD

1 small acorn or butternut squash
3 bell peppers (red, green, yellow, or purple, as available)
1 tablespoon concentrated frozen orange juice
⅓ cup fresh lime juice
¼ cup minced fresh mint *or* 2 tablespoons dried
2 tablespoons toasted and chopped almonds

Cut squash in half and steam over boiling water until tender. Peel, seed, and cut into ½-inch slices. Seed the peppers and cut into julienne strips. Combine the orange juice with lime and mint and toss with peppers. Arrange on serving plate with squash slices and garnish with almonds.

Serves 4

Per serving:	*Calcium* (mg)	*Fat* (g)	*Chol* (mg)	*Carbo* (g)	*Protein* (g)	*Calories*
	52	2.8	0	25.3	4.3	123

YOGURT-STUFFED SQUASH

¼ cup Whole Wheat Bread Crumbs (see index)
1 medium carrot, grated (about 1 cup)
½ teaspoon salt
⅛ teaspoon freshly ground pepper
1 cup sliced mushrooms
1 cup minced onion
1 stalk bok choy, chopped fine (about 1 cup)
½ cup plain low-fat yogurt
2 tablespoons nonfat dry milk
⅛ teaspoon ground cumin
2 acorn or butternut squash, split and seeded

Preheat oven to 350°F. Mix together all the ingredients except the squash and fill the 4 halves with the mixture. Place stuffed squash in a baking dish with a little water in the bottom. Bake for about 40 minutes or until the squash is tender.

Serves 4

Per serving:	*Calcium* (mg)	*Fat* (g)	*Chol* (mg)	*Carbo* (g)	*Protein* (g)	*Calories*
	139	1.3	2	29.9	6.2	144

QUICK SWISS CHARD

2 pound fresh Swiss chard (or collard greens, turnip or mustard greens, beet tops, spinach, or broccoli rabe), well washed, stems trimmed
1 teaspoon salt
1 tablespoon Best Butter (see index)
4 lemon wedges

Trim off any damaged leaves and tough stems of chard. Make sure washing removes all sand. In a saucepan, bring to boil about ½ inch of water and drop in the chard leaves. When the water boils again, cover and cook about 2–3 minutes, until leaves are tender. Add salt and remove from heat. Drain but reserve some of the cooking liquid. Chop the chard, add the Best Butter to the reserved liquid, and pour a little over the chard before serving. Serve each portion with lemon wedge.

Serves 4

Per serving:	*Calcium* (mg)	*Fat* (g)	*Chol* (mg)	*Carbo* (g)	*Protein* (g)	*Calories*
	113	3.4	4	5.4	2.7	57

TOMATO AND CHEESE GRILL

2 large tomatoes
4 ounces part-skim mozzarella cheese, shredded
1 tablespoon olive oil
1 clove garlic, minced
¼ teaspoon dried oregano, crumbled
4 leaves red leaf or romaine lettuce

Cut each tomato into 4 slices and discard stem ends. Place on rack of a broiling pan. Top each tomato slice with an equal portion of cheese and drizzle mixture of oil, garlic, and oregano over each. Preheat broiler and place tomatoes 4 inches from heat. Broil until cheese begins to bubble and brown. Remove and place on bed of lettuce leaves.

Serves 4

Per serving:	*Calcium* (mg)	*Fat* (g)	*Chol* (mg)	*Carbo* (g)	*Protein* (g)	*Calories*
	198	8	16	5	8	122

CREAMED VEGETABLES

2-3 cups any vegetable or combination, such as asparagus, lima beans, peas, cauliflower, broccoli, cabbage, carrots, celery, turnips, green or wax beans, squash, spinach, or kale
1 cup Basic White Sauce (see index)
Almonds and hazelnuts
Curry powder or herbs
Grated cheese

Blanch the vegetables and drain before adding the white sauce and seasonings. Use only a few tablespoons of white sauce with the leafy green vegetables.

Variation: To make baked vegetables au gratin, top the vegetables and white sauce with a covering of fresh bread crumbs or wheat germ, a sprinkling of cheese, and a dash of paprika. Bake in preheated 350°F oven until browned.

Serves 4

Per serving:	*Calcium* (mg)	*Fat* (g)	*Chol* (mg)	*Carbo* (g)	*Protein* (g)	*Calories*
	154	3.3	4	11.2	5	89

STIR-FRY VEGETABLE MEDLEY

1 teaspoon safflower oil
½ teaspoon sesame oil
1 tablespoon low-sodium soy sauce
2 cups shredded red cabbage
1 cup shredded green cabbage
½ cup chopped onion
1 tablespoon finely chopped jalapeño pepper
1 cup broccoli florets
6 leaves spinach or Swiss chard
1 cup Tofu Sauté (see index), cubed
2 tablespoons toasted pumpkin seeds

Heat the oils and soy sauce in large nonstick skillet or wok and stir in the vegetables. Cook quickly over high heat, stirring to blend. Add tofu and pumpkin seeds and toss to combine.

Note: Any other vegetables may be used as desired, such as asparagus or green beans.

Serves 2-3

Per serving:	*Calcium* (mg)	*Fat* (g)	*Chol* (mg)	*Carbo* (g)	*Protein* (g)	*Calories*
	190	10.1	0	13.6	12.7	178

SUMMER SALSA

¼ cup chopped onion
½ cup chopped green bell pepper
½ cup chopped red bell pepper
2 fresh ripe tomatoes, chopped
½ cup fresh lemon juice
Freshly ground black pepper
1 tablespoon chopped fresh basil

Mix all ingredients in a small serving bowl and let stand at room temperature about an hour. Stir occasionally and then refrigerate 1 hour or until serving.

Makes 2 cups or 32 1-tablespoon servings

Per serving:	*Calcium* (mg)	*Fat* (g)	*Chol* (mg)	*Carbo* (g)	*Protein* (g)	*Calories*
	9	.1	0	3.7	.7	16

5
GRAINS, NOODLES, AND POTATOES

Carbohydrates are important in the overall nutritional scheme of things and are necessary for converting our food into energy. High-calcium recipes use brown rice and whole grains such as buckwheat, bulgur, oats, farina, and semolina. The whole grains provide more calcium than refined products. Grains and rice cooked in skim milk provide a lot more calcium.

Potatoes and yams also are vital foods. Whole wheat or vegetable pasta plays a role in this calcium compendium as well. Japanese noodles called *soba* are made of buckwheat flour.

Cook grains and potatoes with a little strip of seaweed for a good calcium and iron boost. Use the skins on potatoes where possible and stuff them with your choice of a creamy filling from Chapters 1, 8, or 12. Wheat germ sprinkled on almost anything is a healthful calcium addition.

Interchange grains for variations on the theme. Prepare them with vegetables, add them to stews, put them in soups, and even use them for desserts.

GRAINS AND NOODLES

BRAZILIAN FAROFA

2 cups skim milk
Pinch salt
⅔ cup farina (Cream of Wheat) or Oat Bran
½ cup chopped onion
2 tablespoons chopped red bell pepper
2 tablespoons chopped green bell pepper
2 tablespoons walnut oil
2 tablespoons wine vinegar

In a nonstick saucepan, bring the milk and salt to a simmer. Slowly add the farina, stirring. Let simmer until thickened, about 10 minutes. In the meantime, mix together the onion, red and green peppers, oil, and vinegar. Serve separately as condiment over farina or Oat Bran.

Serves 6

Per serving:	*Calcium* (mg)	*Fat* (g)	*Chol* (mg)	*Carbo* (g)	*Protein* (g)	*Calories*
	107	4.8	1.3	16.3	4.5	127

BUCKWHEAT GROATS AND VEGETABLES

1 tablespoon safflower oil
2 medium turnips, pared and grated (about 2 cups)
1 medium onion, minced
1 cup sliced mushrooms
½ cup buckwheat groats (kasha)
1 cup skim milk
2 tablespoons nonfat dry milk
2 tablespoons chopped fresh dill *or* 2 teaspoons dried

Heat oil in a nonstick skillet and sauté the vegetables in it. Wash groats, drain, and add to vegetables. Mix and transfer to ovenproof casserole. Combine milks and pour over the mixture and sprinkle with dill. Cover and bake in preheated 350°F oven for 1 hour, or until groats are tender. Fluff and serve.

Serves 6

Per serving:	*Calcium* (mg)	*Fat* (g)	*Chol* (mg)	*Carbo* (g)	*Protein* (g)	*Calories*
	94	2.9	1	12.2	4	89

BULGUR AND VEGETABLE CREAM

1 teaspoon walnut oil
¼ cup chopped onion
1 cup bulgur
½ cup chopped mushrooms
½ cup chopped red cabbage
1 cup grated carrots
1½ cups Chicken Stock or Vegetable Stock (see index)
2 tablespoons chopped dried figs
½ cup plain Yogurt Sour Cream (see index)

Heat oil in nonstick skillet and cook onion in it until soft. Add bulgur and cook until it browns, stirring. Add the vegetables (any combination may be used, such as broccoli, peas, green or red cabbage, or bok choy) and stir again to combine. Add the stock and simmer for 20 minutes, until stock is absorbed. Add the figs and the Yogurt Sour Cream. Stir together. Serve warm or chilled. This can also be used as a base for other foods, such as the crust for broiled mozzarella cheese or a frittata.

Makes about 2½ cups or 6 servings

Per serving:	*Calcium* (mg)	*Fat* (g)	*Chol* (mg)	*Carbo* (g)	*Protein* (g)	*Calories*
	84	1.8	2	29.8	5.2	152

POLENTA AND MUSHROOMS

1 teaspoon olive oil
1 pound mushrooms, cleaned, trimmed, and sliced
2 cups canned Italian plum tomatoes
¼ teaspoon freshly ground pepper
4 cups water, divided
1 cup yellow cornmeal
4 tablespoons nonfat dry milk
4 tablespoons grated Parmesan or sapsago cheese

Heat olive oil in a nonstick skillet and brown the mushrooms in it. Slowly stir in tomatoes and pepper. Simmer 15 minutes over low heat. Meanwhile, bring 3 cups of water to boil in a saucepan. Mix cornmeal with 1 cup of cold water and the nonfat dry milk and gradually stir this into the hot water in the saucepan. Bring back to a boil and cook until thick, stirring constantly. Cover, lower heat, and cook for 10 minutes. Transfer cornmeal to a warm platter, top with the tomato sauce, and sprinkle with grated cheese.

Serves 8

Per serving:	*Calcium* (mg)	*Fat* (g)	*Chol* (mg)	*Carbo* (g)	*Protein* (g)	*Calories*
	67	1.8	2	18.9	4.8	109

ALMOND RICE PILAF

1 cup brown rice (basmati if available)
2 cups Chicken Stock or Vegetable Stock (see index)
½ cup chopped onion
2 tablespoons chopped fresh parsley
2 tablespoons toasted sliced almonds
2 tablespoons grated Parmesan or sapsago cheese
Parsley sprig

Wash rice well under cold water. Bring stock to boil in medium saucepan and add rice, onion, and parsley. Reduce heat and cook, covered, 45 minutes, until done. Mix in almonds and cheese. Garnish with parsley sprig. Use any leftovers for pie crust or rice pudding.

Serves 6

Per serving:	*Calcium* (mg)	*Fat* (g)	*Chol* (mg)	*Carbo* (g)	*Protein* (g)	*Calories*
	38	1.7	1	26.6	3.4	138

RUSSIAN NOODLE PUDDING

8 ounces spinach fettucini
Vegetable spray
1 cup skim milk plus 2 tablespoons nonfat dry milk
1 egg white
1 tablespoon concentrated frozen orange juice
½ cup low-fat cottage cheese
2 tablespoons wheat germ
1 tablespoon caraway seeds
1 tablespoon poppy seeds

Cook noodles in salted boiling water for 12–14 minutes, until just tender. Drain and place in vegetable-sprayed baking pan. In blender, combine milk, egg white, orange juice concentrate, and cottage cheese. Pour over the noodles and sprinkle them with wheat germ and seeds. Bake in preheated 375°F oven for 15 minutes or until golden.

Serves 6

Per serving:	Calcium (mg)	Fat (g)	Chol (mg)	Carbo (g)	Protein (g)	Calories
	93	2.2	39	33	10.2	195

POTATOES

CREAMED POTATOES GRATIN

2 large potatoes, peeled and sliced thin
½ teaspoon salt
Freshly ground pepper
1 cup skim milk
2 tablespoons nonfat dry milk
2 tablespoons part-skim ricotta cheese
2 tablespoons grated Parmesan or sapsago cheese
Paprika

Bring water to boil in the bottom of a double boiler. In the top, cook the potatoes with the salt, pepper, and milks for about 30 minutes. Turn into a baking dish, dot the top with mixture of the ricotta and Parmesan cheeses, and sprinkle with paprika. Bake in preheated 350°F oven for 20 minutes.

Serves 4

Per serving:	Calcium (mg)	Fat (g)	Chol (mg)	Carbo (g)	Protein (g)	Calories
	160	1.5	5.6	15.8	6.2	101

DUTCH TREAT

1 pound fresh kale or cabbage or other green vegetable, chopped fine (about 7 cups)
4 medium potatoes
½ cup nonfat dry milk combined with ¾ cup water
2 cloves garlic, chopped
6 green onions, chopped
½ cup low-fat cottage cheese
¼ teaspoon salt
Freshly ground black pepper to taste
Dash freshly grated nutmeg
Dash cayenne pepper

Rinse the kale well before chopping. Boil potatoes in their jackets until tender. When cooked, slice and return to the saucepan. Spread kale over the potatoes, cover, and steam until tender, about 5–7 minutes. Add remaining ingredients and mash together until well blended.

Serves 6

Per serving:	*Calcium* (mg)	*Fat* (g)	*Chol* (mg)	*Carbo* (g)	*Protein* (g)	*Calories*
	166	.6	2	19.7	8	112

NEW POTATO SALAD

8 small new potatoes, well scrubbed and cooked until tender
1 cup finely chopped celery
¾ cup plain low-fat yogurt
½ cup low-fat cottage cheese
¼ cup white wine vinegar
1 tablespoon Dijon mustard
1 tablespoon fresh lime or lemon juice
1 tablespoon low-sodium soy sauce
Romaine or spinach leaves
1 tablespoon toasted sesame seeds
Tomatoes or other fresh vegetables for garnish

Slice the potatoes into quarters and place in mixing bowl with the celery. Blend together the remaining ingredients except lettuce, sesame seeds, and garnish, then stir into the vegetables. Chill and serve on bed of romaine or spinach leaves. Sprinkle with sesame seeds and garnish with tomatoes or other fresh vegetables.

Serves 6

Per serving:	*Calcium* (mg)	*Fat* (g)	*Chol* (mg)	*Carbo* (g)	*Protein* (g)	*Calories*
	88	1.6	2.6	17	6.3	107

POTATO LEEK PIE

2 medium-size new potatoes, well scrubbed and sliced ¼ inch thick
1 pound leeks, well washed, trimmed, and cut into ½-inch rounds
½ cup Chicken Stock or Vegetable Stock (see index)
Salt and freshly ground black pepper to taste
10 fresh basil leaves, chopped, *or* 1 tablespoon dried, crumbled
Vegetable spray
1 cup sliced mushrooms (about 6 fresh mushrooms)
4 ounces part-skim mozzarella cheese, cubed
Cayenne pepper

Boil potato slices until tender, about 15 minutes. Drain. Cook the leeks in the stock until soft and drain. Toss leeks with salt, pepper, and basil. Coat an ovenproof casserole with vegetable spray. Line the casserole with a layer of the potatoes, then the leeks, then mushrooms, and repeat. Top with cheese, press down and sprinkle with a few dashes of cayenne. Bake, uncovered, for 20 minutes in a preheated 325°F oven.

Serves 6

Per serving:	*Calcium* (mg)	*Fat* (g)	*Chol* (mg)	*Carbo* (g)	*Protein* (g)	*Calories*
	314	3.7	11	14	10.3	120

STUFFED POTATOES

4 medium baking potatoes, well scrubbed
¼ cup plain Yogurt Sour Cream (see note below)
2 tablespoons nonfat dry milk
2 tablespoons grated Parmesan or sapsago cheese
Snipped chives
Paprika

Prick potatoes in several places with a fork and place in a preheated 475°F oven or potato baker. Bake for 1 hour, until shells are very crisp. Remove, cut in half, and scoop out pulp. Mix with Yogurt Sour Cream, dry milk, and cheese. Stuff the shells with the mixture and return to the oven to brown. Serve with a garnish of chives and a dash of paprika.

Note: To make ¼ cup plain Yogurt Sour Cream, follow recipe for Yogurt Sour Cream (see index), using ½ cup plain nonfat or low-fat yogurt.

Serves 4

Per serving:	*Calcium* (mg)	*Fat* (g)	*Chol* (mg)	*Carbo* (g)	*Protein* (g)	*Calories*
	119	1.3	4	21.2	5.7	118

SWISS POTATO TORTE

Vegetable spray
4 medium potatoes, peeled and grated coarse (about 2 cups)
2 small onions, grated
1 cup grated low-fat cheese such as Emmenthaler or part-skim mozzarella
¼ cup grated Parmesan or sapsago cheese
1 teaspoon salt
½ teaspoon freshly ground pepper
⅛ teaspoon freshly grated nutmeg
1 tablespoon chopped fresh parsley
Freshly cooked vegetables

Coat an 8- by 3½-inch round springform pan with vegetable spray. Mix potatoes, onions, cheese, salt, pepper, and nutmeg. Turn into the pan and bake in preheated 450°F oven for 1 hour, until golden brown. Turn the torte out onto a serving platter and garnish with fresh parsley and other freshly cooked vegetables.

Serves 6

Per serving:	*Calcium* (mg)	*Fat* (g)	*Chol* (mg)	*Carbo* (g)	*Protein* (g)	*Calories*
	181	4.1	113	14.9	8	127

TURNIP YAM TREAT

4 turnips, peeled and cubed
2 medium yams, peeled and cubed
¼ cup nonfat dry milk
¼ cup water
Few dashes freshly ground pepper
¼ teaspoon freshly grated nutmeg
Dash dried thyme
2 teaspoons concentrated frozen orange juice

Boil the turnips and yams until tender. Mash together or put through ricer. Add remaining ingredients and stir well together or quickly run through food processor. Adjust seasoning and serve warm. This is especially attractive if served in center of a ring of steamed broccoli.

Serves 4

Per serving:	*Calcium* (mg)	*Fat* (g)	*Chol* (mg)	*Carbo* (g)	*Protein* (g)	*Calories*
	109	.6	1	32.4	3.8	147

6
SALADS

Relatively small amounts of calcium are found in the leafy green vegetables, but when served with a low-fat milk-based dressing, a sprinkling of grated cheese, and a garnish of sesame seeds, soy nuts, or sunflower seeds, they add up to calcium-rich salads. Herbs, parsley, chives, finely chopped or julienned vegetables, and perhaps some crumbled seaweed (that's how the Japanese get their calcium!) will also increase the mineral quantity.

Watercress, dandelion greens (those who live in the country have two seasons for these delicious tender weeds as they proliferate in spring and fall), arugula, romaine lettuce, and raw spinach leaves are all fine combinations for your salad bowl, as is radicchio, a red leaf lettuce that is available in Italian and specialty greengrocers and enhances many dishes.

Salad may be served before or after the main dish, or it may comprise the entire meal. Salad is also a nice complement to a hearty soup dish served with tasty bread or muffins.

BELL PEPPER SALAD

1 medium red bell pepper
1 medium green bell pepper
1 medium yellow or brown bell pepper
½ cup Red Pepper Dressing (see index)
¼ teaspoon freshly ground black pepper
2 teaspoons rinsed and drained capers

Place peppers under broiler and lightly burn, turning to grill all sides. Remove from broiler and drop into a brown paper bag. Close bag and set aside to let steam a few minutes. When cool, peel and core the peppers and cut into strips. Arrange peppers on a platter, alternating colors so that they form a pinwheel, and pour the dressing over them. Sprinkle with ground pepper, garnish with capers, and serve warm or chilled.

Serves 4

Per serving:	*Calcium* (mg)	*Fat* (g)	*Chol* (mg)	*Carbo* (g)	*Protein* (g)	*Calories*
	39	1	1	8.3	2.7	37

CARROT SALAD

2 cups grated unpeeled raw carrots
¼ cup coarsely chopped dried figs
½ cup plain low-fat yogurt
1 tablespoon concentrated frozen orange juice
1 teaspoon fresh lemon juice
1 teaspoon fennel seed
¼ cup chopped fresh parsley
4 romaine lettuce or spinach leaves

Mix carrots with chopped figs. Combine yogurt with orange juice concentrate, lemon juice, fennel seed, and parsley. Mix with carrots and figs. Chill before serving on bed of lettuce or spinach.

Serves 4

Per serving:	*Calcium* (mg)	*Fat* (g)	*Chol* (mg)	*Carbo* (g)	*Protein* (g)	*Calories*
	108	.8	2	19.7	3.1	91

CHICKEN AND CHEESE SALAD

1½ teaspoons minced dried onion
2 tablespoons buttermilk
½ cup plain low-fat yogurt
2 tablespoons part-skim ricotta cheese
¼ cup shredded Jarlsberg or Emmenthaler cheese (1 ounce)
1 teaspoon low-sodium soy sauce
¾ cup diced cooked chicken (or turkey)
½ cup sliced tofu (bean curd), sautéed in nonstick pan
¾ cup sliced bok choy or celery
½ cup shredded carrot
¼ cup chopped green bell pepper
2 tablespoons chopped red bell pepper
8 leaves Swiss chard or spinach
Alfalfa sprouts
1 small ripe tomato, quartered

Soak the dried onion in the buttermilk for 5 minutes, then stir in the yogurt, ricotta, shredded cheese, and soy sauce. Blend well, then combine with diced chicken or turkey. Dice the fried tofu and add along with bok choy, carrot, and green and red peppers. Chill until ready to serve, then spoon onto 4 individual plates lined with chard or spinach leaves. Top with garnish of alfalfa sprouts and place tomato quarters alongside chicken salad. A nice light summer luncheon salad.

Serves 4

Per serving:	*Calcium* (mg)	*Fat* (g)	*Chol* (mg)	*Carbo* (g)	*Protein* (g)	*Calories*
	273	7.4	43.8	8.2	19.2	171

COMPOSED CHEVRE SALAD

6 ounces arugula or watercress, trimmed
6 ounces radicchio or curly red lettuce
1 Belgian endive, leaves separated
1 small navel orange, peeled, seeded, and diced
Few thin rounds or diced pieces of carrot
4 ounces goat cheese
Vegetable spray
Freshly ground black or green pepper
4 tablespoons Balsamic Vinaigrette (see index)

Wash salad greens well and pat dry. Arrange attractively on individual salad plates, strewing the orange and carrot pieces over them. Cut goat cheese into 4 thin slices and place on vegetable-sprayed baking pan. Place under broiler until the cheese begins to melt. Transfer with spatula to top of salads. Sprinkle with pepper and serve with vinaigrette dressing, 1 tablespoon per serving.

Serves 4

Per serving:	*Calcium* (mg)	*Fat* (g)	*Chol* (mg)	*Carbo* (g)	*Protein* (g)	*Calories*
	218	10.3	25	9.5	6.5	151

DANDELION BLUE CHEESE SALAD

1 pound fresh dandelion leaves (young, tender ones)
¼ cup chopped red onion
½ cup Blue Cheese Dressing (see index)
Freshly ground pepper to taste

Wash dandelion greens well in several changes of water and pat dry. Remove coarse stems and tear into 2-inch pieces. Toss with onion and Blue Cheese Dressing and sprinkle with pepper.

Serves 4

Per serving:	*Calcium* (mg)	*Fat* (g)	*Chol* (mg)	*Carbo* (g)	*Protein* (g)	*Calories*
	257	1.8	2.8	12.7	4.7	73

GARBANZO SALAD

1 8-ounce can garbanzos (chick-peas), rinsed and drained
½ cup plain Yogurt Sour Cream (see note below)
2 tablespoons fresh lemon juice
2 cloves garlic, minced
⅛ teaspoon cayenne pepper
3 tablespoons chopped fresh mint *or* 2 teaspoons dried
Salt and freshly ground black pepper to taste
4 romaine, spinach, or fresh chard leaves
Few leaves fresh mint or parsley

Mix the drained garbanzos with the yogurt, lemon juice, garlic, cayenne, mint, and salt and pepper. Chill in covered dish for 1 hour before serving. Place in center of lettuce leaves and garnish with fresh mint or parsley.

Note: To make ½ cup plain Yogurt Sour Cream, follow recipe for Yogurt Sour Cream (see index), using 1 cup plain nonfat or low-fat yogurt.

Serves 4

Per serving:	*Calcium* (mg)	*Fat* (g)	*Chol* (mg)	*Carbo* (g)	*Protein* (g)	*Calories*
	117	1	3.5	10.2	5.3	70

MEXICALI BEAN SALAD

½ pound fresh green beans, blanched
½ cup drained cooked or canned black-eyed peas or kidney beans
6 ounces Mexican-style corn *or* 1 cup fresh corn kernels
½ cup drained cooked lima beans
2 small tomatoes, cored and diced
¼ cup thinly sliced red onion
3 tablespoons fresh lime juice
3 tablespoons white wine vinegar
½ teaspoon crystalline fructose
1 teaspoon garlic powder
½ teaspoon dried oregano, crushed
¼ teaspoon hot red pepper flakes, crushed
6 romaine or spinach leaves
2 tablespoons toasted pumpkin seeds

Mix together first six vegetables and refrigerate for a few hours. Combine remaining ingredients for dressing, except romaine and seeds. When ready to serve, place ½ cup vegetables on greens and serve with dressing and sprinkling of pumpkin seeds.

Serves 6

Per serving:	*Calcium* (mg)	*Fat* (g)	*Chol* (mg)	*Carbo* (g)	*Protein* (g)	*Calories*
	37	1.6	0	16.3	5	93

MEXICAN MIXED SALAD

3 tablespoons red wine vinegar
1 tablespoon Dijon mustard
¼ cup fresh lime juice
Romaine lettuce leaves
1 pound carrots, scraped and grated
1 pound beets, boiled, drained, peeled, and julienned
Beet tops, well washed
1 lime, sliced

Combine vinegar, mustard, and lime juice. Line salad plates with romaine leaves. Fill with equal portions of carrots and beets. Boil beet tops and drain. Place some of these on the lettuce leaves too. Garnish each dish with a lime slice and serve with the lime mustard dressing.

Serves 4

Per serving:	*Calcium* (mg)	*Fat* (g)	*Chol* (mg)	*Carbo* (g)	*Protein* (g)	*Calories*
	81	.8	0	26.5	3.4	114

MIDDLE EAST CUCUMBER SALAD

4 medium cucumbers, peeled, seeded, and sliced thin
Salt
4 cloves garlic, minced
½ cup plain low-fat yogurt
2 tablespoons nonfat dry milk
Dash freshly ground pepper
¼ cup chopped fresh mint leaves *or* 2 tablespoons dried, crumbled

Place cucumbers in a bowl and sprinkle with salt. Let sit, covered, for 1 hour. Rinse, drain, and pat dry. Mix with garlic, yogurt, and nonfat dry milk. Chill and sprinkle with pepper and mint.

Serves 4

Per serving:	*Calcium* (mg)	*Fat* (g)	*Chol* (mg)	*Carbo* (g)	*Protein* (g)	*Calories*
	124	9.7	2.1	10.1	3.8	62

MOZZARELLA MELT

6 cups mixed salad greens such as spinach, radicchio, arugula, curly red lettuce, romaine, and endive leaves
½ cup Creamy Tofu Dressing or Lemon Sauce (see index)
6 ounces part-skim mozzarella cheese
¼ cup wheat germ
1 egg white, beaten
4 teaspoons toasted sesame seeds
Vegetable spray
Dash freshly ground pepper

Arrange salad greens in attractive composition on individual plates. Spoon dressing over leaves. Slice the mozzarella into thin pieces. Spread wheat germ on a plate or on brown paper. Dip cheese slices into the egg white, then coat with wheat germ and top with sesame seeds. Place on vegetable-sprayed baking pan and bake in preheated 325°F oven for 5–10 minutes, until cheese is soft but not entirely melted. Transfer with spatula to top of salad and sprinkle with pepper. This is also a fine main course dish served along with sliced ripe tomatoes and a good Italian whole wheat bread.

Serves 4

Per serving:	*Calcium* (mg)	*Fat* (g)	*Chol* (mg)	*Carbo* (g)	*Protein* (g)	*Calories*
	381	9.6	24	8.6	17.1	179

POTATO SARDINE SALAD

2 cups sliced cooked new potatoes
½ cup Red Pepper Dressing (see index)
Salt and freshly ground pepper to taste
2 cups fresh mustard greens, chard, or watercress
¼ cup shredded Jarlsberg or Emmenthaler cheese
2 3¾-ounce cans water-packed sardines, drained
1 tablespoon chopped fresh parsley

In a small bowl, mix the sliced potatoes with Red Pepper Dressing, season with salt and pepper, and chill, covered, for 1 hour. Place the greens on a serving platter and spread the cheese over them; then layer the potatoes topped with the sardines. Garnish with parsley.

Serves 4

Per serving:	*Calcium* (mg)	*Fat* (g)	*Chol* (mg)	*Carbo* (g)	*Protein* (g)	*Calories*
	269	6.4	58	10.2	12.9	149

RED AND GREEN COLESLAW

1 cup shredded red cabbage
1 cup shredded green cabbage
1 cup chopped celery
1 cup grated raw carrots
1 cup chopped Granny Smith apples
¾ cup plain low-fat yogurt
1 teaspoon fresh lemon juice
2 tablespoons concentrated frozen orange juice
1 teaspoon celery seed
Freshly ground pepper to taste

Combine cabbages, celery, carrots, and apples in a bowl. Mix together yogurt, lemon juice, orange juice concentrate, and celery seed. Mix dressing with vegetables and allow to chill before serving. Season with fresh pepper to taste.

Serves 6

Per serving:	*Calcium* (mg)	*Fat* (g)	*Chol* (mg)	*Carbo* (g)	*Protein* (g)	*Calories*
	85	.6	2	12.1	2.5	60

SARDINES 'N' GREENS

1 3¾-ounce can water-packed sardines including bones, drained
3 tablespoons fresh lime juice
1 teaspoon ground cumin
1 teaspoon dried dill weed
Freshly ground pepper to taste
1 tablespoon sliced scallion
2 tablespoons grated raw carrot
2 tablespoons grated raw zucchini or green cabbage
Romaine, escarole, or spinach leaves
1 tablespoon minced fresh parsley
1 tomato, sliced

Mash sardines with a fork. Mix in the lime juice, ground cumin, dill weed, and pepper to taste. Stir in scallions, carrots, and zucchini or cabbage and adjust seasoning. Serve on bed of greens topped with parsley and surrounded by tomato slices. This makes a luncheon salad or appetizer when served with toasted whole wheat pita bread or rice cakes.

Makes 1 cup sardine mixture or 2 servings

Per serving:	*Calcium* (mg)	*Fat* (g)	*Chol* (mg)	*Carbo* (g)	*Protein* (g)	*Calories*
	238	5.3	68	6.9	12.9	126

SIMPLE SARDINE SALAD

2 cups cauliflower florets
2 cups broccoli florets
2 3¾-ounce cans water-packed sardines including bones, drained
½ cup Creamy Garlic Dressing (see index)
2 tablespoons toasted sesame seeds

Blanch the cauliflower and broccoli florets and run under cold water. Drain. Place in serving bowl. Break up sardines with a fork and put into bowl with vegetables. Spoon dressing over the sardines and vegetables and toss. Let chill until ready to serve. Sprinkle with sesame seeds.

Serves 4

Per serving:	*Calcium* (mg)	*Fat* (g)	*Chol* (mg)	*Carbo* (g)	*Protein* (g)	*Calories*
	220	11.2	51	8.7	14.5	181

SNOW PEA SALAD

2 cups snow peas, trimmed
1 cup julienned red bell pepper
½ cup Creamy Avocado Dressing (see index)
1 teaspoon toasted sesame seeds

Blanch the trimmed snow peas and drain, running under cold water. Pat dry and refrigerate for an hour. When ready to serve, place snow peas in a circle on individual serving plates. Arrange red pepper strips between the pods for a colorful presentation. Spoon dressing over each serving and garnish with sprinkle of sesame seeds.

Serves 4

Per serving:	Calcium (mg)	Fat (g)	Chol (mg)	Carbo (g)	Protein (g)	Calories
	39	1.5	0	6.7	21	43

SPINACH AND NUT SALAD

1 pound fresh spinach
4 scallions, chopped
1 tablespoon walnut oil
½ cup plain low-fat yogurt
1 tablespoon chopped fresh mint *or* 1 teaspoon dried
Salt and freshly ground pepper to taste
1 clove garlic, minced
2 tablespoons chopped almonds and filberts

Wash spinach leaves well and remove tough stems. Chop fine. Combine with scallions and place in large nonstick saucepan. Cook over low heat, stirring until spinach leaves are wilted. Drain. Add walnut oil and toss. Transfer to serving bowl and add yogurt, mint, salt and pepper, and garlic. Chill for 2 hours. Garnish with almonds and filberts.

Serves 4

Per serving:	Calcium (mg)	Fat (g)	Chol (mg)	Carbo (g)	Protein (g)	Calories
	174	6.3	2	9.5	6.2	108

SPINACH AND ORANGE SALAD

2 cups raw spinach
2 navel oranges, peeled and sectioned
½ cup thinly sliced red onion
½ cup Lime and Yogurt Sauce (see index)

Wash spinach leaves well in several changes of water, remove large stems, and pat dry. Tear into bite-size pieces. Add orange sections and onion slices. Toss with sauce, chill, and serve.

Serves 4

Per serving:	*Calcium* (mg)	*Fat* (g)	*Chol* (mg)	*Carbo* (g)	*Protein* (g)	*Calories*
	83	.4	0	11.9	2.6	55

VEGETABLE COTTAGE SALAD

1 cup low-fat cottage cheese
¼ cup chopped fresh parsley
¼ teaspoon salt
Dash freshly ground black pepper
¼ teaspoon toasted sesame seeds
4-6 leaves romaine lettuce, chopped
1 medium ripe tomato, chopped
½ red or green (or combined) bell pepper, seeded and diced
1 small cucumber, cut into spears (peeled if skin is waxy)
2 thin slices red onion

Mix cottage cheese with parsley, salt and pepper, and sesame seeds. Make a bed of chopped romaine and place cottage cheese in its center. Arrange the chopped tomato around the cheese and strew the diced peppers, cucumber spears, and onion around it. Other fresh vegetables may be used as desired.

Serves 2

Per serving:	Calcium (mg)	Fat (g)	Chol (mg)	Carbo (g)	Protein (g)	Calories
	124	1.7	5	11	16.1	126

VEGETABLE SALAD BOWL

2 cups escarole and chicory
2 ripe tomatoes, sliced
½ cup blanched snap beans
½ cup cooked lima beans or kidney beans, rinsed and drained if canned
½ cucumber, peeled and sliced
1 cup sliced zucchini
¼ cup sliced mushrooms
1 cup broccoli florets
2 carrots, cut into julienne strips
½ cup sliced radishes
1 red onion, sliced thin
1 cup Buttermilk Mustard Dressing (see index)

Wash and trim the escarole and chicory and pat or spin dry. Arrange on salad plates and place vegetables over the greens. Spoon Buttermilk Mustard Dressing over each salad.

Serves 6

Per serving:	Calcium (mg)	Fat (g)	Chol (mg)	Carbo (g)	Protein (g)	Calories
	110	.8	1	15.4	5.1	84

WATERCRESS EGG SALAD

2 bunches watercress, trimmed of tough ends, washed, and dried
2 hard-cooked egg whites
2 tablespoons coarsely chopped red onion
4 tablespoons Glorious Green Dressing (see index)
1 tablespoon toasted pumpkin seeds or sesame seeds

Toss watercress, egg whites, and onion with dressing until coated. Serve on individual salad plates with topping of seeds.

Serves 4

Per serving:	*Calcium* (mg)	*Fat* (g)	*Chol* (mg)	*Carbo* (g)	*Protein* (g)	*Calories*
	67	3.1	1	4.8	5.2	63

ZUCCHINI SALAD

1½ pounds zucchini
1 cup plain low-fat yogurt
1 teaspoon fresh lemon juice
1 tablespoon chopped fresh dill
1 tablespoon minced fresh parsley
2 scallions, sliced
½ teaspoon crystalline fructose
Salt and freshly ground pepper to taste
Few dashes paprika

Wash zucchini and slice into thin rounds. Mix well remaining ingredients except paprika and then blend thoroughly with sliced zucchini. Sprinkle top with few dashes of paprika. Chill for a few hours before serving.

Serves 6

Per serving:	*Calcium* (mg)	*Fat* (g)	*Chol* (mg)	*Carbo* (g)	*Protein* (g)	*Calories*
	94	.6	2	6	3	40

7
SALAD DRESSINGS

Dressings are a matter of individual taste. What's sauce for a salad may also be sauce for dessert. Only one dressing in this chapter is oil-based, and that one is intended especially for greens and uses balsamic vinegar. Most of the other milk- or yogurt-based recipes may be used on salad, over vegetables, or with broiled or baked meats, fish, or poultry. Since the milk is universal, many of them double as dessert toppings. For further fun in dressing up any variety of dishes, turn back to the appetizer section and thin out some of these spreads or dips with more milk or even a drop of water. Also refer to Chapter 8, where you'll find sauces that can also be used on salads.

ALMOND GINGER SAUCE

¼ cup toasted almonds, skins removed
¾ cup buttermilk
1 teaspoon grated fresh ginger
½ teaspoon low-sodium soy sauce
Dash salt
2 teaspoons concentrated frozen orange juice

Place almonds in food processor or blender and chop. Add remaining ingredients and blend. Place in saucepan and bring to simmer. Remove from heat. Serve warm over vegetables, fish, or grains or chill and serve over berries or fresh fruit.

Makes 1 cup or 16 1-tablespoon servings

Per serving:	*Calcium* (mg)	*Fat* (g)	*Chol* (mg)	*Carbo* (g)	*Protein* (g)	*Calories*
	18	1.2	0	1.3	.8	18

ANCHOVY YOGURT DRESSING

1 cup plain low-fat yogurt
2 tablespoons safflower or corn oil
¼ cup white wine vinegar
Pinch salt
¼ teaspoon white pepper
1 clove garlic, minced
¼ cup chopped fresh parsley
2 tablespoons anchovies, rinsed
Cayenne pepper

Place all ingredients in a blender and process until smooth. Refrigerate to develop taste. Adjust seasoning before serving. Excellent dressing for vegetables, pasta, fish, salads.

Makes about 1¼ cups or 20 1-tablespoon servings

Per serving:	Calcium (mg)	Fat (g)	Chol (mg)	Carbo (g)	Protein (g)	Calories
	23	1.6	1	1	.7	21

BALSAMIC VINAIGRETTE

1 tablespoon Dijon mustard
¼ cup balsamic vinegar (available in specialty food shops)
2 tablespoons water
2 tablespoons fresh lemon juice
¼ teaspoon dried tarragon
1 clove garlic, minced fine
Salt and freshly ground pepper to taste
¼ cup safflower oil

In a jar, combine the mustard, vinegar, water, lemon juice, tarragon, garlic, and salt and pepper. Shake well to combine. Pour in oil and shake again. Chill before serving.

Makes about ¾ cup or 12 1-tablespoon servings

Per serving:	Calcium (mg)	Fat (g)	Chol (mg)	Carbo (g)	Protein (g)	Calories
	1	3.9	0	.4	.1	37

BLUE CHEESE DRESSING

¼ cup crumbled blue cheese
½ cup plain low-fat yogurt
½ cup buttermilk
½ clove garlic, minced
2 dashes cayenne pepper
Dash freshly ground black pepper
½ teaspoon dried oregano

Blend all ingredients together and refrigerate.

Makes about 1½ cups or 24 1-tablespoon servings

Per serving:	Calcium (mg)	Fat (g)	Chol (mg)	Carbo (g)	Protein (g)	Calories
	21	.5	1	.7	.7	9

BUTTERMILK MUSTARD DRESSING

½ cup buttermilk
¼ cup plain low-fat yogurt
2 teaspoons Dijon mustard
1½ tablespoons peeled, seeded, and grated cucumber
1 tablespoon finely chopped green onion
2 teaspoons chopped fresh parsley
1 teaspoon each grated lemon zest and orange zest
Dash white pepper

Blend all ingredients together and chill before serving.

Makes about ¾ cup or 12 1-tablespoon servings

Per serving:	Calcium (mg)	Fat (g)	Chol (mg)	Carbo (g)	Protein (g)	Calories
	22	.2	1	1	.6	9

CREAMY AVOCADO DRESSING

1 ripe avocado
3 tablespoons fresh lemon juice
¼ cup chopped onion
2 tablespoons seeded and chopped jalapeño pepper
½ cup plain low-fat yogurt
¼ cup evaporated skim milk
Salt and freshly ground black pepper to taste

Scoop pulp out of avocado and place in blender or food processor container. Add lemon juice, onion, and jalapeño pepper. Process to blend. Add yogurt and evaporated milk and process until smooth. Add salt and pepper to taste.

Makes 2 cups or 32 1-tablespoon servings

Per serving:	*Calcium* (mg)	*Fat* (g)	*Chol* (mg)	*Carbo* (g)	*Protein* (g)	*Calories*
	10	1	0	1.2	6	14

CREAMY GARLIC DRESSING

½ cup evaporated skim milk
2 tablespoons strained fresh lemon juice
2 large cloves garlic, minced
¼ teaspoon salt
1 teaspoon dried dill weed
1 teaspoon concentrated frozen apple juice
¼ teaspoon paprika
¼ teaspoon white pepper
2 dashes sesame oil (available in Oriental section of supermarket)
Dash cayenne pepper

Whip all ingredients together in blender until smooth. Chill before serving. Adjust seasoning. Good as salad dressing or topping for tofu.

Makes about ¾ cup or 12 1-tablespoon servings

Per serving:	Calcium (mg)	Fat (g)	Chol (mg)	Carbo (g)	Protein (g)	Calories
	7	.2	0	1	.5	7

CREAMY TOFU DRESSING

1 cup soft tofu (bean curd)
1 large clove garlic, sliced
2 tablespoons low-sodium soy sauce
Juice of 1 lemon with pulp
¼ teaspoon dried oregano
¼ teaspoon dried marjoram
3 tablespoons balsamic vinegar
2 tablespoons chopped scallion
¼ cup water (or as needed)

Place tofu in food processor or blender with remaining ingredients, adding only as much water as needed to make desired consistency.

Makes 2 cups or 32 1-tablespoon servings

Per serving:	Calcium (mg)	Fat (g)	Chol (mg)	Carbo (g)	Protein (g)	Calories
	11	.3	0	.7	.7	8

GLORIOUS GREEN SALAD DRESSING

¼ cup chopped fresh parsley
¼ cup chopped fresh kale, spinach, or chard
1 tablespoon chopped fresh dill weed *or* 1 teaspoon dried
1 cup plain low-fat yogurt
Dash cayenne pepper
Salt and freshly ground black pepper to taste

Blend all ingredients quickly in food processor. Adjust seasoning. Chill before serving.

Variation: Dilute with buttermilk for thinner dressing.

Makes about 1½ cups or 24 1-tablespoon servings

Per serving:	Calcium (mg)	Fat (g)	Chol (mg)	Carbo (g)	Protein (g)	Calories
	19	.2	1	.7	.5	6

HORSERADISH DRESSING-SPREAD

¼ cup plain low-fat yogurt
¼ cup low-fat cottage cheese, rinsed in cold water and drained
1 teaspoon prepared horseradish (sugarless)
¼ teaspoon minced garlic
Dash cayenne pepper

Puree all ingredients together in blender. Nice with fish, on sardines or salads, and as an appetizer.

Makes about ½ cup or 8 1-tablespoon servings

Per serving:	*Calcium* (mg)	*Fat* (g)	*Chol* (mg)	*Carbo* (g)	*Protein* (g)	*Calories*
	18	.2	1	.8	1.3	10

RED PEPPER DRESSING

½ red bell pepper, cored, seeded, and chopped (about ½ cup)
½ fresh tomato, diced (about ¼ cup)
2 chopped fresh basil leaves *or* ½ teaspoon dried
2 tablespoons chopped onions
Dash dried thyme
Dash cayenne pepper
½ teaspoon dried tarragon
Salt and freshly ground black pepper to taste
2 teaspoons balsamic vinegar
1 teaspoon walnut oil
½ cup buttermilk

In a food processor or blender, puree red pepper, tomato, basil, onion, thyme, cayenne, tarragon, and salt and pepper with vinegar and oil. Add buttermilk and stir together. Chill before serving. Delicious served over salads, vegetables, pasta, or broiled fish.

Makes about 1½ cups or 24 1-tablespoon servings

Per serving:	Calcium (mg)	Fat (g)	Chol (mg)	Carbo (g)	Protein (g)	Calories
	7	.2	0	.6	.3	5

RUSSIAN DRESSING

1 cup low-fat cottage cheese, rinsed in cold water and drained
2 tablespoons plain low-fat yogurt
1 tablespoon fresh lemon juice
¼ cup tomato juice
1 tablespoon chopped gherkins
1 hard-cooked egg white, chopped
Salt and freshly ground pepper to taste

Quickly puree cottage cheese, yogurt, and lemon juice in a blender, then add the tomato juice. Stir in the gherkins and egg white by hand and season with salt and pepper. Refrigerate before serving.

Makes about 1¼ cups or 20 1-tablespoon servings

Per serving:	Calcium (mg)	Fat (g)	Chol (mg)	Carbo (g)	Protein (g)	Calories
	8	.1	1	.6	1.3	9

TOMATO VELOUTE

½ cup evaporated skim milk
¼ teaspoon Dijon mustard
¼ teaspoon salt
Freshly ground pepper
2 tablespoons tarragon vinegar
2 tablespoons fresh lemon juice
¼ cup tomato juice
1 tablespoon minced fresh parsley

Chill the milk. Combine mustard, salt, pepper, vinegar, and lemon juice. Stir the tomato juice into the chilled milk, then add the vinegar-lemon mixture gradually, stirring until blended. Add parsley, adjust seasoning, and blend well.

Makes 1 cup or 16 1-tablespoon servings

Per serving:	*Calcium* (mg)	*Fat* (g)	*Chol* (mg)	*Carbo* (g)	*Protein* (g)	*Calories*
	6	0	0	.8	.4	5

WATERCRESS DRESSING

1 cup watercress leaves, well washed
½ cup part-skim ricotta cheese
⅔ cup buttermilk
1 tablespoon nonfat dry milk
3 tablespoons chopped scallion
1 tablespoon anchovy paste
1 teaspoon white wine vinegar
1 teaspoon fresh lemon juice
¼ teaspoon dried tarragon, crushed
Salt and freshly ground pepper to taste

In a food processor, chop the watercress leaves, then add remaining ingredients and blend. Chill and serve over vegetables.

Makes 2 cups or 32 1-tablespoon servings

Per serving:	*Calcium* (mg)	*Fat* (g)	*Chol* (mg)	*Carbo* (g)	*Protein* (g)	*Calories*
	19	.4	1	.7	.7	9

YOGURT MAYONNAISE FINES HERBES

6 tablespoons plain low-fat yogurt
2 tablespoons (or less) tarragon vinegar
2 tablespoons low-sodium soy sauce
1 tablespoon chopped herbs, such as fresh basil, parsley, dill, oregano
½ teaspoon chopped onion
1 sliver garlic, minced
½ teaspoon Dijon mustard
Salt and freshly ground pepper

Mix all ingredients together well and chill before serving to blend flavors. Excellent dressing for coleslaw, vegetables, broiled fish or meat.

Variation: For a thinner dressing, add buttermilk as desired.

Makes ¾ cup or 12 1-tablespoon servings

Per serving:	*Calcium* (mg)	*Fat* (g)	*Chol* (mg)	*Carbo* (g)	*Protein* (g)	*Calories*
	18	.2	0	1.1	.7	8

8
SAUCES

Yogurt, buttermilk, evaporated skim milk, nonfat dry milk, and tofu may be used as bases for original and imaginative sauces. Add fruit, seeds or nuts, carob, coffee, molasses, or juice or make your own combinations. These add flair and flavor to desserts and baked goods, and some may even be used as salad dressings, according to individual taste. They all add calcium in a tasteful way.

Goat's milk, kefir, and soy milk may be substituted, for those with a lactose intolerance or merely for a change of taste.

CURRY SAUCE

1 teaspoon corn oil
1 onion, minced
1-2 teaspoons curry powder
½ cup plain low-fat yogurt
½ teaspoon salt

In nonstick skillet, heat oil and cook onion in it. Stir in curry powder and add yogurt and salt. Simmer for about 2 minutes, stirring. Serve over vegetables, fish, or chicken.

Makes ½ cup or 8 1-tablespoon servings

Per serving:	*Calcium* (mg)	*Fat* (g)	*Chol* (mg)	*Carbo* (g)	*Protein* (g)	*Calories*
	29	.8	1	2.1	.9	19

LEMON SAUCE

1 lemon, washed, unpeeled, cut into pieces
2 dashes sesame oil
1 cup soft tofu (bean curd)
½ cup buttermilk
½ teaspoon prepared horseradish
1 teaspoon Dijon mustard
¼ teaspoon salt
Freshly ground pepper to taste
1 tablespoon chopped black olives (optional)

Place lemon pieces in blender or food processor with the oil and blend until lemon is cut into small pieces. Add remaining ingredients and blend until smooth. Chill and serve as dip for fresh vegetables or as dressing for artichokes, fish, or even grains.

Makes 2 cups or 32 1-tablespoon servings

Per serving:	Calcium (mg)	Fat (g)	Chol (mg)	Carbo (g)	Protein (g)	Calories
	12	1.2	.1	.6	.6	14

LIME AND YOGURT SAUCE

2 tablespoons fresh lime juice
2 tablespoons water
⅛ teaspoon salt
Dash freshly ground pepper
¼ cup plain low-fat yogurt

Stir together first 4 ingredients. Add yogurt and blend. Delicious over fresh fruit.

Makes ½ cup or 8 1-tablespoon servings

Per serving:	Calcium (mg)	Fat (g)	Chol (mg)	Carbo (g)	Protein (g)	Calories
	13	.1	0	.7	.4	5

MANGO CHEESE SAUCE

1 mango, pulp pureed to make 1 cup
½ cup part-skim ricotta cheese
¼ cup low-fat cottage cheese
1 teaspoon fresh lemon juice

Blend all ingredients until smooth in a food processor. Serve over fresh fruit or baked goods. Also tasty over some salads. Makes a great sauce for a banana split or peach melba.

Makes about 2 cups or 32 1-tablespoon servings

Per serving:	Calcium (mg)	Fat (g)	Chol (mg)	Carbo (g)	Protein (g)	Calories
	13	.3	1	1.5	.8	12

MISSISSIPPI MUD SAUCE

¼ cup carob powder
1 tablespoon crystalline fructose
½ cup evaporated skim milk
¼ cup chunky peanut butter
¼ teaspoon pure vanilla extract

In a small saucepan, stir together the carob, fructose, and milk and bring to simmer. Remove from heat, beat in peanut butter with a wire whisk, and add vanilla. Stir until combined. This gets slightly thicker as it chills. Use as sauce for fruits, cream desserts, or even a bread such as the Orange Ginger Bread (see index).

Makes about ½ cup or 8 1-tablespoon servings

Per serving:	*Calcium* (mg)	*Fat* (g)	*Chol* (mg)	*Carbo* (g)	*Protein* (g)	*Calories*
	19	2.5	0	4.1	1.9	39

PAPAYA PUREE

1 ripe papaya
¼ cup evaporated skim milk
2 tablespoons nonfat dry milk
Dash white pepper
⅛ teaspoon pure vanilla extract
¼ teaspoon grated fresh ginger

Peel papaya and scoop out pulp. Save seeds for garnish. Place papaya pulp in blender or food processor and puree. Add remaining ingredients. This is a multipurpose sauce! If using for simply cooked chicken, fish, or veal, heat before serving. Chill if using as a dessert sauce over fruit.

Makes 1 cup or 16 1-tablespoon servings

Per serving:	Calcium (mg)	Fat (g)	Chol (mg)	Carbo (g)	Protein (g)	Calories
	12	0	0	2.4	.4	11

POPEYE PESTO

1 pound fresh spinach, well rinsed, tough stems trimmed
½ cup plain low-fat yogurt
½ cup low-fat cottage cheese
¼ cup grated Parmesan cheese
2 tablespoons dried basil
¼ cup chopped almonds
2 cloves garlic
¼ cup chopped fresh parsley, stems removed

Steam spinach lightly in just the water remaining on leaves. Drain. Combine all ingredients in food processor or blender until smooth. Serve over pasta, warm or chilled.

Makes about 2 cups or 32 1-tablespoon servings

Per serving:	Calcium (mg)	Fat (g)	Chol (mg)	Carbo (g)	Protein (g)	Calories
	38	.9	1	1.5	1.6	19

POPPY SEED SAUCE

1 cup plain low-fat yogurt
2 teaspoons grated orange zest
1 teaspoon grated lemon zest
2 tablespoons raspberry or apple cider vinegar
1 tablespoon concentrated frozen orange juice
3 tablespoons poppy seeds

Stir all ingredients together until well blended. Refrigerate for several hours to develop taste. Refreshing served over fresh fruit or fruit salads.

Makes about 1¼ cups or 20 1-tablespoon servings

Per serving:	*Calcium* (mg)	*Fat* (g)	*Chol* (mg)	*Carbo* (g)	*Protein* (g)	*Calories*
	40	.8	1	1.5	.9	16

RICOTTA PEANUT BUTTER

¼ cup chunky peanut butter
½ cup evaporated skim milk
½ cup part-skim ricotta cheese
1 teaspoon ground cinnamon
2 teaspoons concentrated frozen orange juice
1 teaspoon toasted sesame seeds

Mix all ingredients together, stirring well to blend. Refrigerate before serving. Use as topping for potatoes or casseroles, over noodles or rice, or as a snack or appetizer.

Makes 1 cup or 16 1-tablespoon servings

Per serving:	*Calcium* (mg)	*Fat* (g)	*Chol* (mg)	*Carbo* (g)	*Protein* (g)	*Calories*
	26	2.6	2	1.6	2.1	37

SAUCY ORANGE CHIFFON

½ cup evaporated skim milk
3 ounces part-skim ricotta cheese
¼ cup concentrated frozen orange juice
1 tablespoon chopped fresh mint, *or* ½ teaspoon dried, crushed

Place all ingredients in a blender and process until smooth. Chill before serving. Delicious over fruit or baked goods. Topped with cut chives, parsley, or basil, it is also tasty served over turkey, veal, chicken, fish, and salads or vegetables.

Makes about 1 cup or 16 1-tablespoon servings

Per serving:	*Calcium* (mg)	*Fat* (g)	*Chol* (mg)	*Carbo* (g)	*Protein* (g)	*Calories*
	21	.4	2	2.4	1	17

VIENNA CREAM SAUCE

½ cup plain low-fat yogurt
½ cup part-skim ricotta cheese
1½ tablespoons blackstrap molasses
3 tablespoons chopped hazelnuts and almonds
2 tablespoons chopped dried figs

Mix the yogurt and ricotta together until smooth. Add the remaining ingredients and chill until ready to serve. Spoon over fresh fruits—particularly piquant served over sliced bananas as a split! Also something special over baked treats.

Makes about 1½ cups or 24 1-tablespoon servings

Per serving:	*Calcium* (mg)	*Fat* (g)	*Chol* (mg)	*Carbo* (g)	*Protein* (g)	*Calories*
	31	1.1	2	2.6	1.1	23

YOGURT FRUIT SAUCE

½ cup plain Yogurt Sour Cream (see note below)
4 teaspoons sugar-free fruit conserve

Stir together yogurt and fruit conserve and chill 30 minutes or more. Delightful topping for fruits, cakes, or crackers.

Note: To make ½ cup plain Yogurt Sour Cream, follow recipe for Yogurt Sour Cream (see index), using 1 cup plain nonfat or low-fat yogurt.

Makes about ¾ cup or 12 1-tablespoon servings

Per serving:	*Calcium* (mg)	*Fat* (g)	*Chol* (mg)	*Carbo* (g)	*Protein* (g)	*Calories*
	35	.3	1	2.1	1	15

9
BREADS AND MUFFINS

Baked goods are a prime way to provide calcium. Most folks have their own favorite breads, puddings, soufflés, and baked desserts. By adding more nonfat dry milk or substituting skim milk, buttermilk, or evaporated skim milk for whole milk products and cheese, you can give your recipes a substantial calcium boost. Baking may also be done with kefir, soy milk, and goat's milk for those who cannot digest lactose. The addition of raisins, chopped figs or dates, sesame seeds, sunflower or pumpkin seeds, almonds, and filberts gives more flavor and crunch, and more calcium, too.

Some of these recipes may double as dessert served with a creamy dessert sauce, and some as a main course. Whether the goodies are mini muffins or soufflés, high-calcium baking is a boon!

BREADS

BOSTON BROWN BREAD

½ cup whole wheat flour
½ cup all-purpose unbleached flour
¼ cup cornmeal
1 tablespoon wheat germ
½ teaspoon baking powder
¼ teaspoon baking soda
¼ teaspoon salt
1 egg, beaten
¼ cup blackstrap molasses
1 tablespoon crystalline fructose
2 tablespoons nonfat dry milk
2 teaspoons safflower oil
¾ cup buttermilk
2 tablespoons sunflower seeds
3 tablespoons raisins
Vegetable spray

Stir together flours, cornmeal, wheat germ, baking powder, baking soda, and salt. In another bowl, combine egg, molasses, fructose, dry milk, and oil. Add the flour mixture to the liquid, alternating with addition of the buttermilk. Beat together well. Stir in sunflower seeds and raisins. Coat 2 16-ounce empty cans with cooking spray and turn batter into them in equal portions. Cover tightly with foil and place in a large Dutch oven. Pour boiling water into the kettle to a depth of 1 inch and bring back to boil. Reduce heat, cover, and simmer over low heat for about 3 hours, until bread tests done (when toothpick inserted in center comes out clean). Add more water to the kettle if needed. Lift cans from pan and let stand 10 minutes on a wire rack before removing breads. Serve warm with Crème Fraîche or Whipped Ricotta Cream (see index).

Makes 2 loaves, each about 7 slices

Per slice:	Calcium (mg)	Fat (g)	Chol (mg)	Carbo (g)	Protein (g)	Calories
	49	2	20	15.3	2.7	87

BUTTERMILK SODA BREAD

1 cup whole wheat flour
1 cup plus 1 tablespoon all-purpose unbleached flour
¼ cup wheat germ
2 tablespoons crystalline fructose
2 teaspoons baking soda
2 teaspoons double-acting baking powder
½ teaspoon salt
2 cups buttermilk
1½ tablespoons safflower oil
2 tablespoons toasted sunflower seeds
2 tablespoons chopped dried figs
Vegetable spray

Stir all dry ingredients together in large bowl, then add buttermilk and oil until batter is blended but still lumpy. Add sunflower seeds and chopped figs and mix. Coat a 9-inch round pan with vegetable spray and dust with extra all-purpose flour. Spoon batter into the pan and bake in preheated 375°F oven for 50–60 minutes, until a toothpick inserted in the center comes out clean. Cool bread for 10 minutes in pan, then turn out on wire rack. Cut into wedges to serve.

Makes about 16 servings

Per serving:	Calcium (mg)	Fat (g)	Chol (mg)	Carbo (g)	Protein (g)	Calories
	54	2.4	1	16	3.4	97

CAROB-NUT BREAD PUDDING

¼ cup unsweetened carob powder
6 tablespoons water
3 cups skim milk
3 tablespoons concentrated frozen orange juice
⅛ teaspoon salt
2 eggs (1 yolk only)
2 tablespoons part-skim ricotta cheese
½ teaspoon ground cinnamon
Vegetable spray
4 slices day-old or toasted whole wheat bread, processed to rough cubes in blender (the better the bread, the better the pudding!)
¼ cup chopped almonds and hazelnuts

Sift carob powder into a mixing bowl and stir in the water until smooth. Add milk, orange juice concentrate, salt, eggs, ricotta, and cinnamon and blend together in blender or food processor. Coat two 4- by 8-inch loaf pans with vegetable spray and line with bread crumbs. Over this pour the carob mixture, stir, and let stand about 20 minutes to absorb the liquid. Stir. Top with nuts. Preheat oven to 350°F and place the loaf pans in another pan containing 1 inch of hot water. Bake for about 50–60 minutes or until a toothpick inserted in the middle comes out clean.

Serves 8–10

Per serving:	*Calcium* (mg)	*Fat* (g)	*Chol* (mg)	*Carbo* (g)	*Protein* (g)	*Calories*
	165	3.8	37.4	17.1	7.1	120

CHILI-CHEESE CORNBREAD

1¼ cups yellow or blue cornmeal
2 teaspoons baking powder
½ teaspoon baking soda
½ teaspoon salt
¼ cup whole wheat flour
1¼ cups buttermilk
2 eggs (1 yolk only), beaten lightly
¼ cup shredded sharp cheddar cheese or Formagg
2 tablespoons chopped mild green chilies (more or less as desired)
Vegetable spray

Sift together into a large bowl 1 cup plus 2 tablespoons of cornmeal and the baking powder, soda, salt, and flour. Stir in the buttermilk, eggs, cheese, and chilies, combining well. Coat an 8-inch square baking pan with vegetable spray and sprinkle it with remaining 2 tablespoons of cornmeal. Turn the batter into the pan and bake in upper third of preheated 450°F oven for 10 minutes or until it is firm in center.

Makes about 12 2-inch servings

Per serving:	*Calcium* (mg)	*Fat* (g)	*Chol* (mg)	*Carbo* (g)	*Protein* (g)	*Calories*
	54	1.5	23	12.5	3.2	76

COTTAGE OAT BREAD

1½ cups whole wheat flour
2 tablespoons active dry yeast
3 tablespoons minced onion
½ cup hot water
2 cups low-fat cottage cheese
2 tablespoons walnut oil
½ cup nonfat dry milk
1 teaspoon salt
2 tablespoons crystalline fructose
2 eggs (1 yolk only)
1 cup quick-cooking or rolled oats
2 tablespoons dill seeds or fennel
2 teaspoons caraway seeds
1½ cups all-purpose unbleached flour
Vegetable spray

Place the whole wheat flour and yeast in large bowl of an electric mixer. In food processor or blender, combine the onion, water, cottage cheese, walnut oil, dry milk, salt, fructose, and eggs. Process until smooth. Turn into the bowl of flour and beat for 2 minutes. Then stir in the oats, seeds, and unbleached flour. Coat a large bowl with vegetable spray and turn the mixture into it. Cover and let rise in a warm place for about an hour or until doubled in bulk. Punch down, place in a greased 1½-quart casserole, and let rise, uncovered, for 45 minutes or until again twice its bulk. In the meantime, preheat oven to 350°F. Bake 1 hour or until the loaf sounds hollow when tapped.

Makes 1 large loaf, 12–14 slices

Per slice (12 slices):	*Calcium* (mg)	*Fat* (g)	*Chol* (mg)	*Carbo* (g)	*Protein* (g)	*Calories*
	76	4.2	25	31.6	12.2	210

Per slice (14 slices):	*Calcium* (mg)	*Fat* (g)	*Chol* (mg)	*Carbo* (g)	*Protein* (g)	*Calories*
	55	3.6	21.4	27.1	10.5	180

GREEN AND RED CABBAGE BREAD

Vegetable spray
1 teaspoon fresh lemon juice
½ cup finely shredded red cabbage
½ cup finely shredded green cabbage
½ cup plain low-fat yogurt
1 egg
¼ cup concentrated frozen orange juice
¼ cup nonfat dry milk
¼ cup safflower oil
1 cup whole wheat flour
¾ cup all-purpose unbleached flour
¼ cup toasted sesame seeds
2 teaspoons baking powder
½ teaspoon baking soda
⅛ teaspoon ground mace
⅛ teaspoon ground ginger

Preheat oven to 350°F. Coat a loaf pan with vegetable spray. Mix lemon juice with red and green cabbage and set aside. Mix yogurt with egg, orange juice concentrate, dry milk, and oil, blending well. Then add cabbage. Mix the remaining dry ingredients together thoroughly. Gradually pour the wet mixture into the dry and mix to blend. Pour into loaf pan and bake 35–45 minutes, until browned and tester comes out clean when inserted in middle of loaf. Remove and let cool on rack.

Serves 10

Per serving:	*Calcium* (mg)	*Fat* (g)	*Chol* (mg)	*Carbo* (g)	*Protein* (g)	*Calories*
	75	8.3	28	20.5	5.4	174

NORWEGIAN NUT BREAD

1 cup sifted all-purpose unbleached flour
1 teaspoon baking soda
1 teaspoon salt
½ cup chopped almonds, filberts, and sunflower seeds
¼ cup nonfat dry milk
1 cup unsifted whole wheat flour
½ cup raisins
1 tablespoon grated orange zest
1 beaten egg
1 cup buttermilk
2 tablespoons walnut oil
Vegetable spray

Preheat oven to 375°F. Measure sifted flour into a mixing bowl with baking soda and salt. Add nuts, dry milk, whole wheat flour, and raisins. Combine orange zest, egg, buttermilk, and walnut oil and stir into the flour mixture until well blended. Coat 2 16-ounce empty cans with vegetable spray and spoon mixture into them. Bake for 50 minutes or until golden. Loosen around edges with a spatula and turn onto rack to cool. Serve with Low-Fat Cream Cheese or Make-Believe Mayo (see index).

Makes 2 small loaves, about 6 slices each

Per slice:	*Calcium* (mg)	*Fat* (g)	*Chol* (mg)	*Carbo* (g)	*Protein* (g)	*Calories*
	65	5	24	22.7	5.9	151

ORANGE GINGER BREAD

1 package active dry yeast
½ cup warm water or warmed yogurt whey (see index)
¼ teaspoon ground ginger
½ teaspoon crystalline fructose
3 tablespoons concentrated frozen orange juice
1 teaspoon caraway seeds
1 teaspoon salt
2 tablespoons grated orange zest
2 tablespoons walnut oil
12 ounces evaporated skim milk
1 cup rye flour
Freshly ground pepper
2 cups all-purpose unbleached flour
½ cup nonfat dry milk
Vegetable spray

In a large mixing bowl, dissolve yeast in warm water or whey. Blend in ginger and fructose. Let stand until yeast foams, about 5 minutes. Add orange juice concentrate, caraway seeds, salt, orange zest, oil, and evaporated skim milk. Add the rye flour and black pepper and mix until batter is smooth. Gradually add the all-purpose flour and nonfat dry milk, mixing until smooth and satiny. Turn into 2 vegetable-sprayed casseroles (about 1 quart each) and let rise, covered, in a warm place until dough doubles or fills the dish. Bake in preheated 350°F oven for 50–60 minutes or until a toothpick inserted into the center comes out clean. Let cool a few minutes, then remove and cool on rack.

Makes 2 loaves, about 12 wedges each

Per wedge:	*Calcium* (mg)	*Fat* (g)	*Chol* (mg)	*Carbo* (g)	*Protein* (g)	*Calories*
	82	2.6	0	30	5.7	167

SESAME BREAD

1 cup low-fat cottage cheese
1 package active dry yeast
¼ cup warm water
1 tablespoon crystalline fructose
¼ teaspoon baking soda
1 egg, beaten
4 tablespoons toasted sesame seeds
¼ cup nonfat dry milk
1 teaspoon salt
1 scant cup whole wheat flour
1 scant cup all-purpose unbleached flour
2 tablespoons wheat germ
Vegetable spray

Heat the cottage cheese until just warm. Soften the yeast in the warm water. After 5 minutes, add the yeast mixture to the cottage cheese, then add the fructose, soda, egg, sesame seeds, nonfat dry milk, and salt and mix well. Turn into a bowl. Combine the flours and wheat germ and gradually add to the cottage cheese mixture, stirring to blend. Cover and let stand in a warm place for a few hours, until doubled in bulk. Stir down to original size and turn into a vegetable-sprayed loaf pan. Cover with a cloth and again let stand to double for about an hour. Bake in preheated 350°F oven for 40 minutes. Loaf is done when it sounds hollow when tapped. Let cool in refrigerator before slicing. Nice when toasted, too.

Makes one loaf, about 16–18 slices

Per slice:	*Calcium* (mg)	*Fat* (g)	*Chol* (mg)	*Carbo* (g)	*Protein* (g)	*Calories*
	16	1.7	16	10.6	4.1	72

SHARP CHEDDAR BREAD

1 package active dry yeast
¼ cup warm water or yogurt whey
½ teaspoon crystalline fructose
1 tablespoon safflower oil
¾ cup skim milk plus 2 tablespoons nonfat dry milk
½ cup plain low-fat yogurt
¼ cup grated sharp cheddar cheese or low-fat Formagg cheese substitute
1 teaspoon salt
1 cup all-purpose unbleached flour
2 cups whole wheat flour
Vegetable spray
1 tablespoon dill seed
1 tablespoon toasted sesame seeds

Dissolve yeast in warm water or whey with fructose. Stir in the oil, milks, yogurt, cheese, and salt. Add the all-purpose flour, beating to blend, and then gradually stir in the whole wheat flour until dough is stiff. Turn onto a floured board and knead for 5 minutes. Add more whole wheat flour if necessary (oil hands for this task—it is a sloppy one!). Place dough in a bowl coated with vegetable spray, turning to coat the dough. Cover and let rise in a warm place until doubled in size. Punch down and form into a loaf. Put into a 4- by 8-inch loaf pan also coated with cooking spray. Cover and let rise until doubled in bulk, about 1 hour. Sprinkle top of loaf with seeds. Bake in preheated 375°F oven for 50 minutes.

Makes 1 loaf, about 16 slices

Per slice:	*Calcium* (mg)	*Fat* (g)	*Chol* (mg)	*Carbo* (g)	*Protein* (g)	*Calories*
	54	2.2	3	17.6	4.3	105

MUFFINS

JOAN'S GOURMET MUFFINS

1 cup buttermilk
1 egg
1½ tablespoons walnut oil
1 cup all-purpose unbleached flour
¼ cup whole wheat flour
1 teaspoon baking powder
½ teaspoon baking soda
¼ teaspoon salt
6 tablespoons grated Parmesan or sapsago cheese
½ teaspoon dried rosemary, crushed
Vegetable spray

Beat together the buttermilk, egg, and oil. In another large bowl sift together the flours, baking powder, soda, and salt. Combine grated cheese and rosemary in a separate dish. Add 4 tablespoons of the grated cheese with the rosemary mixed in and toss with a fork to blend. Pour the buttermilk mixture into the center of the flour and combine with fork until blended but still lumpy. Coat 2 mini-muffin tins with vegetable spray and spoon the mixture into the cups, filling any empty ones with water. Top each muffin cup with sprinkling of remaining cheese and rosemary and place in upper third of preheated 350°F oven for 20–25 minutes until toothpick inserted in center comes out clean. Muffins should be nicely browned.

Makes 20 mini muffins

Per muffin:	*Calcium* (mg)	*Fat* (g)	*Chol* (mg)	*Carbo* (g)	*Protein* (g)	*Calories*
	65	1.9	15.4	6.2	2.2	51

MAGIC MUFFINS

Vegetable spray
1¼ cups whole wheat flour
1 cup oat bran
1 tablespoon wheat germ
½ cup nonfat dry milk
1 tablespoon sunflower seeds
3 tablespoons raisins
1 teaspoon baking powder
1 teaspoon crystalline fructose
2 tablespoons safflower oil
2 tablespoons concentrated frozen orange juice
⅔ cup grated carrot
½ teaspoon ground cinnamon
½ teaspoon ground nutmeg

Coat muffin tin with vegetable spray. Preheat oven to 400°F. In a large mixing bowl, combine ingredients through fructose, and in a smaller bowl mix the remaining ingredients. Combine both mixtures well and turn into sprayed muffin cups. Bake for 30 minutes.

Makes 12 large muffins

Per muffin:	*Calcium* (mg)	*Fat* (g)	*Chol* (mg)	*Carbo* (g)	*Protein* (g)	*Calories*
	37	3.2	0	16.4	3.7	108

OAT BRAN MUFFINS

Vegetable spray
2¼ cups oat bran cereal
2 tablespoons crystalline fructose
¼ cup chopped almonds
2 tablespoons chopped dried figs
1 teaspoon baking powder
½ teaspoon salt
¼ cup concentrated frozen orange juice
¾ cup buttermilk
1 egg
1 egg white
2 tablespoons vegetable oil

Coat muffin tin with vegetable spray or line with paper baking cups. Combine all dry ingredients. Add remaining ingredients and mix together well. Fill muffin tins about three-fourths full and bake in preheated 425°F oven for about 15 minutes, until golden.

Makes about 18 muffins

Per muffin:	*Calcium* (mg)	*Fat* (g)	*Chol* (mg)	*Carbo* (g)	*Protein* (g)	*Calories*
	30	2.4	16	7.8	2.8	51

PARMESAN POPOVERS

Vegetable spray
4 egg whites at room temperature
⅓ cup plus 2 tablespoons nonfat dry milk
1 cup water
¾ cup all-purpose unbleached flour
¼ cup whole wheat flour
2 tablespoons Best Butter (see index)
⅛ teaspoon freshly grated nutmeg
6 teaspoons grated Parmesan or sapsago cheese

Preheat oven to 450°F and coat a 12-cup muffin tin or 6 custard cups with vegetable spray. Place all ingredients except the cheese in blender or food processor and blend for 15–20 seconds, being careful not to overmix. Pour batter into the muffin tin or custard cups. Sprinkle each muffin cup with ½ teaspoon of the grated cheese or use 1 teaspoon on each custard cup. Bake batter in the muffin tin for 15 minutes or in the custard cups for 20 minutes. Reduce heat to 350°F and bake each for the same amount of time at the lower heat. Remove and serve at once.

Makes 6 large or 12 small muffins

Per small muffin:	*Calcium* (mg)	*Fat* (g)	*Chol* (mg)	*Carbo* (g)	*Protein* (g)	*Calories*
	43	2.4	4	8.7	3.3	70

Per large muffin:	*Calcium* (mg)	*Fat* (g)	*Chol* (mg)	*Carbo* (g)	*Protein* (g)	*Calories*
	86	4.8	8	17.4	6.6	140

10
DESSERTS

Ice cream is usually the prescription for women who need extra calcium. But the eggs and sugar and heavy cream that make up this rich dessert negate its benefits. The "ice creams" found in this chapter are more truly ice milks or sherbets. They are easily made of skim milk, yogurt, or buttermilk with fruits, carob, cocoa, nuts, and spices. A simple ice cream maker or just a metal ice tray and a blender or food processor are the only tools needed.

Some low-fat custards and mousses are also included on the following pages, as are a few delicious cream pies. Throughout the year you can enjoy desserts using summer berries by simply freezing them and storing them for later use. Combine them or any fruit with low-fat yogurt, kefir, part-skim ricotta, or any of the recipes in the chapters on sauces or basics that appeal to you. Buttermilk is a wonderful base for a cold fruit soup so popular in Scandinavia. The Perfect Pie Crust or Graham Cracker Crust in Chapter 12 may be filled with a myriad of choices for calcium-rich delicious desserts.

FROZEN DESSERTS

ALMOND APPLE ICE CREAM

1 apple, cored and diced
1 frozen banana
1 envelope nonfat dry milk
1 cup water
1 tablespoon concentrated frozen orange juice
½ teaspoon pure vanilla extract
1 teaspoon instant regular or decaf coffee
1 tablespoon blanched slivered almonds
Dash freshly grated nutmeg

Blend all ingredients except last 2 in food processor. Pour into metal trays and place in freezer, stirring periodically and processing again before serving. Top with almonds and a dash of nutmeg.

Serves 4

Per serving:	*Calcium* (mg)	*Fat* (g)	*Chol* (mg)	*Carbo* (g)	*Protein* (g)	*Calories*
	74	1.4	1	16.7	27	84

BANANA MAPLE ICE CREAM

1 cup evaporated skim milk
2 cups sliced frozen bananas
½ teaspoon imitation maple flavoring
2 tablespoons chopped hazelnuts and almonds

Pour evaporated milk into metal tray and place in freezer for about an hour. Slice frozen bananas, place in food processor with the frozen milk, and blend until smooth and creamy. Add maple flavoring and blend again. Return to metal tray and stir in the nuts. Cover with foil and replace in freezer. Take out to stir with a fork from time to time before serving. This is best served at once or not more than 1 hour after refreezing.

Serves 4

Per serving:	*Calcium* (mg)	*Fat* (g)	*Chol* (mg)	*Carbo* (g)	*Protein* (g)	*Calories*
	89	2.4	0	21.1	5.9	115

BANANA TOFU ICE CREAM

6 ounces tofu (bean curd)
2 medium frozen bananas, sliced
4 ice cubes, crushed or shaved
1 teaspoon crystalline fructose
1 teaspoon blackstrap molasses
¼ teaspoon freshly grated nutmeg
¼ cup nonfat dry milk
½ cup water
½ teaspoon pure vanilla extract (or more to taste)
1 tablespoon chopped almonds and hazelnuts

Place all ingredients except nuts in food processor and blend until smooth. Place in bowl in freezer for a short time and then transfer to refrigerator before serving. This is a puddinglike cream and may even be eaten immediately following preparation. Do not let it freeze hard. Sprinkle a few chopped nuts over each serving.

Serves 4

Per serving:	*Calcium* (mg)	*Fat* (g)	*Chol* (mg)	*Carbo* (g)	*Protein* (g)	*Calories*
	122	3.4	1	17.9	5.9	116

FUDGE FREEZE

1 cup skim milk
2 eggs (1 yolk only)
1 egg white
1 teaspoon pure vanilla extract
¼ cup carob powder
2 tablespoons nonfat dry milk
1 teaspoon instant regular or decaf coffee
2 teaspoons crystalline fructose
Dash salt
1 tablespoon roughly chopped hazelnuts

Heat the milk in a small saucepan to scald and remove from heat. Place remaining ingredients except hazelnuts in a blender. Cover and process on slow, then remove cover and pour in hot milk. Process again for about a minute. Turn into metal tray and place in freezer, stirring periodically to break up ice crystals. Stir in hazelnuts before serving.

Serves 4

	Calcium (mg)	*Fat* (g)	*Chol* (mg)	*Carbo* (g)	*Protein* (g)	*Calories*
Per serving:	231	2.5	70	11.1	5.8	81

ORANGE MIST

1 cup freshly squeezed orange juice
2 teaspoons fresh lemon juice
1 teaspoon grated orange zest
1 cup evaporated skim milk

Mix together orange and lemon juices and orange zest. Pour into metal tray and place in freezer for 1–2 hours, stirring periodically. Pour the milk into a small metal bowl and put in freezer along with the beaters of an electric mixer. Remove after an hour, when crystals have begun to form. Quickly beat until the milk is whipped into stiff peaks. Remove orange freeze and beat separately for a minute. Then fold into the whipped milk and return to freezer for about 30–45 minutes before serving in sherbet glasses. Do not make this too far ahead.

Serves 4

Per serving:	*Calcium* (mg)	*Fat* (g)	*Chol* (mg)	*Carbo* (g)	*Protein* (g)	*Calories*
	82	0	0	13.9	5	78

PAPAYA PISTACHIO CREAM

1 ripe papaya, peeled and seeded (reserve some seeds for garnish)
1 cup plain low-fat yogurt
½ teaspoon pure vanilla extract
1 teaspoon fresh lime juice
1 teaspoon grated orange zest
Ground cinnamon
2 tablespoons peeled and chopped pistachios

Place papaya pulp in food processor and puree with yogurt. Add vanilla, lime juice, and orange zest. Pour into metal tray and place in freezer, stirring frequently. Do not leave in freezer longer than 1–2 hours. Spoon out onto dessert dishes and garnish with cinnamon and nuts, plus papaya seeds if desired. May be served immediately rather than frozen.

Serves 4

Per serving:	*Calcium* (mg)	*Fat* (g)	*Chol* (mg)	*Carbo* (g)	*Protein* (g)	*Calories*
	127	2.9	4	12.5	4.2	88

PEACH FREEZE

2 cups peeled, pitted, and mashed fresh peaches
1 cup plain low-fat or nonfat yogurt
1 teaspoon pure vanilla extract
2 tablespoons unflavored gelatin
2 tablespoons concentrated frozen orange juice
1 tablespoon grated orange zest
Toasted sesame seeds
Ground cinnamon

Combine peaches, yogurt, and vanilla until well mixed. Sprinkle the gelatin over the orange juice concentrate and wait 5 minutes before dissolving the gel over hot water. Then combine with peach mixture. Place in metal tray, cover, and put in freezer for about 1 hour, stirring periodically. Do not allow this to freeze solid. Before serving, stir again, spoon into 4 dessert glasses, and top with grated orange zest, sesame seeds, and cinnamon.

Serves 4

Per serving:	*Calcium* (mg)	*Fat* (g)	*Chol* (mg)	*Carbo* (g)	*Protein* (g)	*Calories*
	112	1.3	4	17.1	7	103

PINEAPPLE GINGER FROGURT

1 cup plain low-fat yogurt
½ cup crushed unsweetened canned pineapple
1 teaspoon grated fresh ginger
½ banana
1 teaspoon crystalline fructose
½ teaspoon pure vanilla extract
1 tablespoon sunflower seeds

Combine all ingredients except sunflower seeds and blend in a food processsor until smooth. Turn into metal tray and place in freezer. After 30 minutes or so, scrape sides and stir to break up crystals. Repeat. Do not leave in the freezer longer than an hour or two before serving. May also be prepared in ice cream maker. Sprinkle with sunflower seeds before serving.

Serves 4

Per serving:	*Calcium* (mg)	*Fat* (g)	*Chol* (mg)	*Carbo* (g)	*Protein* (g)	*Calories*
	112	2	4	15.5	3.8	91

CANTALOUPE SHERBET

3 cups peeled, seeded, and cubed cantaloupe
1 cup nonfat dry milk
2 tablespoons concentrated frozen orange juice
2 cups water
¼ teaspoon freshly grated nutmeg
1 teaspoon pure vanilla extract
½ teaspoon ground cinnamon
2 tablespoons fresh lemon juice

Place cantaloupe in food processor and puree. Add remaining ingredients and process until blended. Turn into metal trays and put in freezer, stirring every so often to break up crystals. Process again before serving. May be used as dessert, served with sliced fruits, or on waffles or ladyfingers.

Serves 6

Per serving:	Calcium (mg)	Fat (g)	Chol (mg)	Carbo (g)	Protein (g)	Calories
	149	.3	2	14.0	4.7	75

ICED MOCHA SHERBET

1½ cups evaporated skim milk
1 teaspoon pure vanilla extract
2 tablespoons carob powder
1 tablespoon crystalline fructose
2 tablespoons concentrated frozen orange juice
1 tablespoon instant coffee or decaf
1 tablespoon part-skim ricotta cheese

Mix all ingredients together in blender and turn into metal trays. Place in freezer and stir with fork from time to time to break up ice crystals. When ready to serve, process again so that sherbet is soft.

Serves 4

Per serving:	Calcium (mg)	Fat (g)	Chol (mg)	Carbo (g)	Protein (g)	Calories
	121	.5	1	27.2	7.1	101

PURPLE SHERBET

1 cup chopped, seeded MacIntosh apple
1 cup natural grape juice
½ cup nonfat dry milk
½ teaspoon pure vanilla extract

Place all ingredients in blender or food processor and puree until frothy. Pour into metal trays and place in freezer, stirring often to break up ice crystals. Process again before serving.

Serves 6

Per serving:	*Calcium* (mg)	*Fat* (g)	*Chol* (mg)	*Carbo* (g)	*Protein* (g)	*Calories*
	75	.2	1	12.8	2.3	60

CUSTARDS, MOUSSES, AND PUDDINGS

COFFEE CUSTARD CUPS

2 eggs (1 yolk only)
1 cup evaporated skim milk
1 teaspoon instant regular or decaf coffee
½ teaspoon pure vanilla extract
1 tablespoon concentrated frozen orange juice
1 tablespoon grated orange zest
Ground cinnamon

Process eggs in blender, then add evaporated milk, instant coffee, vanilla, and orange juice concentrate. Pour into 4 individual custard cups and place in a larger baking pan filled with about 1 inch of boiling water. Bake in preheated 350°F oven for 45 minutes or until a knife inserted in the center comes out clean. Remove from oven, chill, run a knife around edges of cups, invert, and garnish each custard with sprinkling of orange zest and cinnamon.

Serves 4

Per serving:	*Calcium* (mg)	*Fat* (g)	*Chol* (mg)	*Carbo* (g)	*Protein* (g)	*Calories*
	47	1.4	66	8.9	7.1	80

PEANUT CUSTARD

2 tablespoons peanut butter
1 cup evaporated skim milk, divided
2 eggs (1 yolk only)
½ teaspoon pure vanilla extract
4 teaspoons chopped roasted peanuts

Stir together the peanut butter and ½ cup of the milk in a small bowl. In a separate bowl, whisk the eggs and add the remaining milk, then the peanut butter mixture and vanilla. Turn into a small ovenproof baking dish or into 4 individual custard cups and place in a larger pan containing about an inch of boiling water. Bake in preheated 350°F oven for about 45 minutes or until a knife inserted in the center comes out clean. Cool, turn out onto dessert dishes, and serve garnished with peanuts.

Serves 4

Per serving:	*Calcium* (mg)	*Fat* (g)	*Chol* (mg)	*Carbo* (g)	*Protein* (g)	*Calories*
	91	7.2	69	9.4	10	142

ALMOND DELIGHT

2 teaspoons walnut oil
½ cup blanched almonds
⅓ cup semolina grain
1½ cups skim milk
2 tablespoons nonfat dry milk
3 teaspoons crystalline fructose
½ teaspoon pure vanilla extract
2 tablespoons chopped dried figs, plumped in water

Heat walnut oil in large nonstick skillet. Sauté almonds in it for 2–3 minutes. Add semolina grain and cook, stirring, until lightly browned. In another small saucepan, bring skim milk, dry milk, and fructose to boil. Pour this into the semolina and almond pan and stir. Let simmer a few minutes, until thick. Add vanilla extract and drained figs, stir, and serve warm in dessert dishes.

Serves 4

Per serving:	*Calcium* (mg)	*Fat* (g)	*Chol* (mg)	*Carbo* (g)	*Protein* (g)	*Calories*
	191	11.4	2	23	8	217

CAROB CREAM

1 teaspoon unflavored gelatin
¼ cup cold water
4 tablespoons carob powder
Pinch salt
1 cup evaporated skim milk, divided
1 egg yolk, beaten
½ teaspoon pure vanilla extract
2 tablespoons chopped almonds and hazelnuts

Sprinkle gelatin over cold water until firm. Then place over a bowl of hot water to dissolve. In a saucepan, combine carob powder, salt, the dissolved gelatin, and half of the milk and mix until blended. Add egg yolk and stir together over low heat until thick. Stir in vanilla extract with wire whisk. Remove from heat and let cool. In the meantime, pour remaining milk into a metal bowl and place in freezer for an hour, until crystals form around edges. Also place the beaters of an electric mixer in freezer to chill. When cold enough, beat until stiff. Then fold the carob mixture into the whipped milk and beat together until peaks form. Serve at once in sherbet dishes or place in freezer for 30 minutes before serving. This does not hold and needs to be made close to mealtime. It might also be served with a scattering of fruit. Top with nuts before serving.

Serves 4

Per serving:	*Calcium* (mg)	*Fat* (g)	*Chol* (mg)	*Carbo* (g)	*Protein* (g)	*Calories*
	120	3.6	68	14.3	7.9	108

APRICOT MOUSSE

½ cup dried apricots, dried prunes, or a combination
½ cup soft tofu (bean curd)
2 teaspoons pure vanilla extract
2 tablespoons nonfat dry milk
2 egg whites at room temperature
Fresh mint leaves (optional)

Soak fruits in hot water for 30 minutes, then drain. Drain the soft tofu between paper towels and turn into the container of a food processor or blender along with the fruit, vanilla, and dry milk. Process. Whip the egg whites until stiff but not dry. Pour fruit mixture into a bowl and fold egg whites into it. Spoon into dessert glasses, garnish with mint, and serve chilled.

Makes about 1 cup or 2 ½-cup servings

Per serving:	*Calcium* (mg)	*Fat* (g)	*Chol* (mg)	*Carbo* (g)	*Protein* (g)	*Calories*
	136	2.6	0	12.8	9.8	106

MANGO MOUSSE

2 ripe mangoes or papaya (2 cups pulp)
1 cup hulled and rinsed fresh strawberries
½ teaspoon pure vanilla extract
1½ cups evaporated skim milk
1 tablespoon concentrated frozen orange juice

Puree all ingredients in food processor or blender and pour into metal trays. Place in freezer and stir every 30 minutes or so to break up ice crystals. Blend again before serving.

Makes 4 cups or 6 ⅔-cup servings

Per serving:	Calcium (mg)	Fat (g)	Chol (mg)	Carbo (g)	Protein (g)	Calories
	92	.6	0	29.3	5.6	137

BANANA BERRY RICE PUDDING

1 cup cooked brown rice
½ cup mashed banana
½ cup nonfat dry milk
¾ cup water
1 teaspoon maple extract
1 teaspoon ground cinnamon
1 teaspoon toasted sesame seeds
¼ cup concentrated frozen orange juice
2 tablespoons fresh blueberries *or* 1 tablespoon raisins
2 egg whites, beaten stiff
1 tablespoon sunflower seeds

Mix together all ingredients except egg whites and sunflower seeds. Fold egg whites into rice mixture and pour into 4-inch by 8-inch baking pan. Top with sprinkling of sunflower seeds. Bake in preheated 350°F oven for 1 hour or until pudding is set.

Serves 6

Per serving:	Calcium (mg)	Fat (g)	Chol (mg)	Carbo (g)	Protein (g)	Calories
	81	1	1	19.9	4.7	106

BANANA SWEET POTATO PUDDING

½ pound sweet potatoes, peeled and cubed (about 1 cup)
¼ cup water
2 medium bananas, sliced
1 cup skim milk mixed with 2 tablespoons nonfat dry milk
½ teaspoon coconut extract
1 small cinnamon stick
1 tablespoon concentrated frozen orange juice
½ teaspoon pure vanilla extract
2 tablespoons slivered almonds

Boil the sweet potatoes in water for 20 minutes or until tender. Drain off any excess water and add bananas, milk, coconut extract, cinnamon stick, and orange juice concentrate. Cook about 15 minutes or until thick. Remove cinnamon stick and add vanilla. Puree in blender or food processor and serve either warm or chilled, topped with slivered almonds.

Serves 6

Per serving:	*Calcium* (mg)	*Fat* (g)	*Chol* (mg)	*Carbo* (g)	*Protein* (g)	*Calories*
	90	1.8	1	24.4	3.6	123

COFFEE CREAM PUDDING

1 envelope unflavored gelatin
¼ cup concentrated frozen orange juice
1 cup strong freshly brewed regular or decaf coffee
1 tablespoon crystalline fructose
1 cup low-fat cottage cheese
¼ cup part-skim ricotta cheese
1 egg, separated
4 tablespoons sugarfree fruit conserve (raspberry, peach, or any flavor desired)
12 almonds and filberts

In a small bowl, sprinkle the gelatin on the concentrated orange juice. Add coffee and fructose. Stir to dissolve gelatin. Place cottage cheese and ricotta in food processor container, drop in egg yolk, and process. Add gelatin mixture and repeat. Pour into metal tray and place in freezer for no more than 30 minutes, so that it does not freeze. In the meantime, whip the egg white until it is stiff. Remove cottage cheese mixture from freezer and fold in egg white. Turn into individual molds or 1 3-cup ring mold. Into the center of each portion place ½ tablespoon of the fruit conserve. Refrigerate until set. When ready to serve, unmold by dipping in hot water for a second or loosening with a sharp knife. Top with remaining fruit conserve and some nuts. May also be served with orange slices or other fresh fruit.

Serves 4

Per serving:	*Calcium* (mg)	*Fat* (g)	*Chol* (mg)	*Carbo* (g)	*Protein* (g)	*Calories*
	78	3.3	76	13.9	12.3	132

FRUIT DESSERTS

BERRIES AND YOGURT A L'ORANGE

1 cup plain low-fat yogurt
⅛ teaspoon freshly grated nutmeg
⅛ teaspoon ground mace
½ teaspoon finely chopped orange zest
1 pint strawberries, halved or sliced
1 pint blackberries or blueberries
4 twists of orange peel

Mix yogurt with the spices and chopped orange zest. Chill. Wash and trim the berries. Divide berries among 4 parfait glasses or dessert dishes and top with the yogurt sauce. Garnish each with orange twist.

Note: Any fruit may be substituted, such as peaches, bananas, plums, nectarines, orange segments, kiwifruit, melon, etc.

Serves 4

Per serving:	*Calcium* (mg)	*Fat* (g)	*Chol* (mg)	*Carbo* (g)	*Protein* (g)	*Calories*
	118	1.5	3.5	19.5	3.9	99

MEDITERRANEAN MELON

½ teaspoon ground cinnamon (or more to taste)
1 cup plain Yogurt Sour Cream (see note below)
2 cups peeled, seeded, and cubed honeydew melon or cantaloupe
2 tablespoons chopped almonds and filberts
Mint sprigs

Stir cinnamon into the yogurt and adjust to taste. Mix the melon with the yogurt and nuts and serve chilled in dessert glasses with a sprig of mint as garnish.

Note: To make 1 cup plain Yogurt Sour Cream, follow recipe for Yogurt Sour Cream (see index), using 2 cups plain low-fat or nonfat yogurt.

Serves 4

Per serving:	*Calcium* (mg)	*Fat* (g)	*Chol* (mg)	*Carbo* (g)	*Protein* (g)	*Calories*
	224	4.1	7	14.4	7.3	118

PEACH MELBA

4 large ripe peaches
1 cup plus 2 tablespoons raspberries
½ cup part-skim ricotta cheese
2 tablespoons nonfat dry milk plus water to make ¼ cup
1 tablespoon grape juice

Blanch peaches by dropping them into boiling water for 30 seconds. Remove, run under cold water, and peel off skins. Cut in half, discard pits, and place 2 peach halves on each of 4 individual dessert dishes. Puree raspberries with remaining ingredients, reserving 2 tablespoons of berries for garnish. Spoon puree over peaches, top with berries, and serve cold.

Serves 4

Per serving:	*Calcium* (mg)	*Fat* (g)	*Chol* (mg)	*Carbo* (g)	*Protein* (g)	*Calories*
	120	2.7	10	16.5	5.1	104

RASPBERRY PARFAIT

1 envelope unflavored gelatin
¼ cup cold water
10 ounces frozen unsweetened raspberries, thawed
1 cup plain low-fat yogurt
½ teaspoon pure vanilla extract
2 egg whites at room temperature
1 teaspoon crystalline fructose
1 tablespoon slivered blanched almonds

In a mixing bowl, soften the gelatin in cold water and then place over hot water to dissolve. Stir in the raspberries, yogurt, and vanilla and chill. In the meantime, beat egg whites until frothy and add the fructose. Beat again until peaks form, then fold into the raspberry mixture. Chill until set. Serve in parfait glasses, topped with slivered almonds.

Serves 4–6

Per serving:	*Calcium* (mg)	*Fat* (g)	*Chol* (mg)	*Carbo* (g)	*Protein* (g)	*Calories*
	119	2.3	4	9.8	6	77

RED, WHITE, AND BLUE BAKE

12 ounces farmer cheese
¼ cup pineapple juice (or more as needed)
½ teaspoon salt (or more to taste)
6 rings unsweetened canned pineapple slices
¾ cup fresh blueberries
½ cup sliced fresh strawberries
Vegetable spray
1 tablespoon toasted sunflower seeds
Pinch ground cinnamon
1 cup Saucy Orange Chiffon (see index)

Crumble farmer cheese and mix with pineapple juice and salt. Cube the pineapple rings, keeping 2 whole for garnish. Reserve some berries for garnish and mix remainder into cheese. Spray 4- by 8-inch loaf pan and turn in cheese and fruit. Pat down firmly and top with extra berries, pineapple, sunflower seeds, and cinnamon. Bake in preheated 350°F oven for 20 minutes. Remove, let cool for 30 minutes, and chill in refrigerator for 1½ hours. Cut around edges with a spatula and transfer loaf to serving dish. Slice and serve with other fruits or crisp crackers and Saucy Orange Chiffon if desired.

Note: Other combinations of fruit may be used, such as peaches, bananas, plums, and raisins.

Serves 8

Per serving without sauce:	*Calcium* (mg)	*Fat* (g)	*Chol* (mg)	*Carbo* (g)	*Protein* (g)	*Calories*
	71	1.1	2	13.7	6.8	90

RUSSIAN RHUBARB

1 pound rhubarb, washed and trimmed
¼ cup concentrated frozen orange juice
2 tablespoons water
2 tablespoons crystalline fructose
1 cup sliced strawberries
Crème Fraîche (see index)

Soak rhubarb in cold water for 10 minutes. Drain, slice into chunks, and place in saucepan with orange juice concentrate, 2 tablespoons water, and fructose. Simmer, covered, for 10–15 minutes, until soft and stringy. Add strawberries, stir, chill, and serve with dollop of Crème Fraîche.

Serves 4

Per serving:	*Calcium* (mg)	*Fat* (g)	*Chol* (mg)	*Carbo* (g)	*Protein* (g)	*Calories*
	260	3	10	19	6	124

STUFFED FIGS

12 large dried figs, split horizontally
24 blanched almonds
¼ cup Crème Fraîche or Saucy Orange Chiffon (see index)

Soak figs in hot water to soften for about 30 minutes. Drain and pat dry. Stuff each fig with 2 almonds and pinch closed. Arrange on cookie sheet and bake in preheated 325°F oven for 10 minutes. Remove and serve at room temperature with a dollop of Crème Fraîche or Saucy Orange Chiffon.

Makes 12 servings

Per serving:	*Calcium* (mg)	*Fat* (g)	*Chol* (mg)	*Carbo* (g)	*Protein* (g)	*Calories*
	55	3.6	1.6	13.6	2.2	88

WHITE FRUIT DELIGHT

2 teaspoons unflavored gelatin
3 tablespoons unsweetened canned pineapple juice
2 cups low-fat cottage cheese
4 tablespoons nonfat dry milk
½ orange, peeled, pitted, and diced
½ cup sliced strawberries
½ cup blueberries
½ cup Grapenuts
2 tablespoons sunflower seeds

Soften gelatin in pineapple juice and after 5 minutes heat over hot water to dissolve. Mix together with cottage cheese and nonfat dry milk in a blender or food processor. In the meantime arrange the fruit in an attractive pattern in bottom of an 8-inch metal mold. Pour the cottage cheese mixture over the fruit, cover, and refrigerate for a few hours. When ready to serve, immerse mold in a little warm water to loosen. Turn upside down onto a serving dish and garnish with Grapenuts and sunflower seeds.

Serves 8

Per serving:	*Calcium* (mg)	*Fat* (g)	*Chol* (mg)	*Carbo* (g)	*Protein* (g)	*Calories*
	72	1.8	3	11.8	9.1	98

PIES AND TARTS

CAROB CREAM PIE

1 Graham Cracker Crust (see index)
1 cup part-skim ricotta cheese
1 cup plain Yogurt Sour Cream (see note below)
2 teaspoons carob or cocoa powder
½ teaspoon pure vanilla extract
6 hazelnuts
6 almonds
Dash ground cinnamon
Fresh berries (optional)

Bake crust as directed and let cool. Place ricotta and yogurt in a large bowl with carob powder and vanilla and beat together with electric mixer until smoothly blended. Turn into the baked pie shell, decorate the top with an arrangement of the nuts, and refrigerate until firm. Top with dusting of cinnamon and a fresh berry or two if available.

Note: To make 1 cup plain Yogurt Sour Cream, follow recipe for Yogurt Sour Cream (see index) using 2 cups plain nonfat or low-fat yogurt.

Serves 8

Per serving:	*Calcium* (mg)	*Fat* (g)	*Chol* (mg)	*Carbo* (g)	*Protein* (g)	*Calories*
	194	8.6	13	11	7.4	148

KIWI LIME PIE

1 cup plain Yogurt Sour Cream (see note below)
1 cup part-skim ricotta cheese
2 tablespoons crystalline fructose
1 teaspoon concentrated frozen orange juice
½ teaspoon pure vanilla extract
Juice of two limes
1 baked Graham Cracker Crust (see index)
2 kiwifruit, peeled and sliced into thin rounds (or use thinly sliced oranges)

When yogurt is drained and all whey removed (save for use in soups or breads), place in mixing bowl with ricotta cheese, fructose, orange juice concentrate, vanilla, and lime juice. Beat with electric mixer until creamy. Pour into pie shell and chill until set. Before serving, arrange fruit slices so that they overlap each other in a decorative pattern.

Note: To make 1 cup plain Yogurt Sour Cream, follow recipe for Yogurt Sour Cream (see index), using 2 cups plain nonfat or low-fat yogurt.

Serves 8

Per serving:	*Calcium* (mg)	*Fat* (g)	*Chol* (mg)	*Carbo* (g)	*Protein* (g)	*Calories*
	197	7.5	13	16.2	7.4	157

MOCHA FILLING

1 cup part-skim ricotta cheese
1 teaspoon ground cinnamon
1½ teaspoons carob powder
2 tablespoons crystalline fructose
½ teaspoon pure vanilla extract
2 tablespoons chopped almonds

Blend all ingredients except almonds in food processor and add a little skim milk for desired consistency, if necessary. Top with almonds and serve on ladyfingers, graham crackers, or in pie made from Perfect Pie Crust (see index).

Serves 6

Per serving:	*Calcium* (mg)	*Fat* (g)	*Chol* (mg)	*Carbo* (g)	*Protein* (g)	*Calories*
	160	4.8	13	14.4	5.4	101

RICOTTA RAISIN TARTS

½ cup raisins
¼ cup port wine
1 cup part-skim ricotta cheese
1 tablespoon grape juice
2 teaspoons grated lemon zest
Pinch salt
½ teaspoon pure vanilla extract
¼ cup chopped almonds and hazelnuts
1 recipe Perfect Pie Crust dough (see index)

Plump raisins in wine for about 2 hours and then pour into a small saucepan and cook until liquid has evaporated. Mix cheese with the grape juice, lemon zest, salt, and vanilla. Stir in the cooled raisins and nuts. Meanwhile, make the dough, roll thin, and cut into 8 rounds (use a cup or a glass), and shape to fit into an 8-cup muffin tin. Bake crust in preheated 350°F oven for 20–30 minutes, until brown. Remove from oven and let cool. These may be made ahead and kept in the freezer. Stuff with ricotta mixture and return to oven for 10 minutes. Let cool, remove from tins, and serve.

Serves 8

Per serving:	*Calcium* (mg)	*Fat* (g)	*Chol* (mg)	*Carbo* (g)	*Protein* (g)	*Calories*
	108	10	10	22.2	6.9	205

11
BEVERAGES

Some soft drinks now have added calcium, but the caffeine and other chemicals and additives also in these drinks negate any benefits. The drinks you can make at home are infinite in their variety, from the simplest "egg cream" of seltzer, skim milk, and coffee to Hot Russians and cinnamon cocoa or a health drink of yogurt, blackstrap molasses, and wheat germ. Goat's milk, kefir, and soy milk—even CalciMilk for the lactose intolerant—will combine in a shake. Buttermilk, yogurt, tofu, frozen bananas, berries, orange juice, skim milk, and combinations of some dessert sherbets blended with ice cubes will yield smooth and nourishing beverages with punch. Many of these shakes are delicious breakfast alternatives—blended with your favorite cereal, bran, or wheat germ. Others serve as a great snack or relaxing bedtime beverage.

Simple mineral waters are laden with calcium: Mountain Valley, produced in California, contains a hefty 380 mg of calcium per liter! The Italian San Pellegrino water has more than 200 mg per liter, Ferrarelle 446 mg per liter, and French Contrexeville has 451 per liter. If your tap water is hard, chances are it is high in calcium, too. Cheers!

COLD DRINKS

ALMOND CAROB MILK SHAKE

¼ cup blanched almonds
2 tablespoons carob powder
2 cups skim milk
2 tablespoons nonfat dry milk
¼ teaspoon pure vanilla extract
4 tablespoons crushed ice

Process almonds in blender until they are ground fine. Add remaining ingredients and blend until frothy.

Serves 4

Per serving:	*Calcium* (mg)	*Fat* (g)	*Chol* (mg)	*Carbo* (g)	*Protein* (g)	*Calories*
	214	4.7	2.1	118	6.6	106

EGGNOG

1 egg white
1½ cups skim milk
½ cup nonfat dry milk
½ teaspoon crystalline fructose
½ teaspoon pure vanilla extract
4 ice cubes, crushed
¼ teaspoon freshly grated nutmeg

Blend all ingredients except nutmeg at high speed for 30 seconds. Garnish with dusting of nutmeg.

Serves 4

Per serving:	*Calcium* (mg)	*Fat* (g)	*Chol* (mg)	*Carbo* (g)	*Protein* (g)	*Calories*
	438	.4	6	18	13.9	134

FIZZY STRAWBERRY FREEZE

1 cup frozen unsweetened strawberries
1 cup skim milk
2 tablespoons nonfat dry milk
½ teaspoon crystalline fructose
½ cup cold seltzer

Puree all ingredients except the seltzer in a blender. Pour into 2 tall glasses and add half the seltzer to each glass for a frothy fruit drink.

Serves 2

Per serving:	*Calcium* (mg)	*Fat* (g)	*Chol* (mg)	*Carbo* (g)	*Protein* (g)	*Calories*
	212	.5	3	13.3	6.1	80

FRAN'S FRAPPE

1 cup buttermilk
¼ cup nonfat dry milk
½ cup fresh blueberries or strawberries
½ teaspoon fructose
4 ice cubes, crushed
Extra berries

Blend all ingredients together and pour into 2 tall glasses. Garnish each with a whole strawberry or a few blueberries.

Serves 2

Per serving:	*Calcium* (mg)	*Fat* (g)	*Chol* (mg)	*Carbo* (g)	*Protein* (g)	*Calories*
	250	1.3	6	15.4	7.3	100

FROZEN BANANA SHAKE

1 frozen banana
2 tablespoons carob powder
2 tablespoons nonfat dry milk
2 cups skim milk
1 tablespoon wheat germ
4 ice cubes, crushed

Cut frozen banana into chunks. Place all ingredients in blender or food processor and blend until smooth.

Serves 4

Per serving:	*Calcium* (mg)	*Fat* (g)	*Chol* (mg)	*Carbo* (g)	*Protein* (g)	*Calories*
	192	.5	2.5	17.5	5.7	87

HAPPY HEALTH SHAKE

1 cup plain low-fat yogurt
1 tablespoon blackstrap molasses
2 teaspoons wheat germ

Whip all ingredients together in a blender and pour into 2 tall frosted glasses.

Serves 2

Per serving:	*Calcium* (mg)	*Fat* (g)	*Chol* (mg)	*Carbo* (g)	*Protein* (g)	*Calories*
	287	1.9	7	14.6	6.8	100

MELON MIXER

1 cup cubed cantaloupe or honeydew melon
½ cup plain low-fat yogurt
½ cup skim milk
½ teaspoon freshly grated nutmeg
1 tablespoon concentrated frozen orange juice
Mint sprig
Small wedge lemon

Blend together all ingredients but mint and lemon, which should be used for garnish.

Serves 2

Per serving:	*Calcium* (mg)	*Fat* (g)	*Chol* (mg)	*Carbo* (g)	*Protein* (g)	*Calories*
	187.5	1.1	4.5	14.5	5.7	89

MOCHA MILK SHAKE

1 tablespoon instant regular or decaf coffee
2 tablespoons carob powder
2 tablespoons nonfat dry milk
2 cups skim milk
4 ice cubes, crushed

Place all ingredients in blender or food processor and mix until frothy. Pour into 2 chilled glasses.

Serves 2

Per serving:	*Calcium* (mg)	*Fat* (g)	*Chol* (mg)	*Carbo* (g)	*Protein* (g)	*Calories*
	381	.5	5	20.5	10.2	115

ORANGE BRACER

1 cup freshly squeezed orange juice
1 egg white
½ cup nonfat dry milk
½ teaspoon pure vanilla extract
2 ice cubes, crushed
2 orange slices

Blend all ingredients but orange slices at high speed and serve in frosted glasses, garnished with orange slices.

Serves 2

Per serving;	Calcium (mg)	Fat (g)	Chol (mg)	Carbo (g)	Protein (g)	Calories
	89	.2	1	16.6	4.6	86

PEACHY SLIM NOG

½ cup skim milk
2 tablespoons nonfat dry milk
1 cup sliced fresh peaches
1 tablespoon concentrated frozen apple juice
¼ teaspoon freshly grated nutmeg

Blend all ingredients except nutmeg until smooth and frothy. Garnish with dusting of nutmeg.

Serves 1

Per serving:	Calcium (mg)	Fat (g)	Chol (mg)	Carbo (g)	Protein (g)	Calories
	260	.4	3	27.2	7.7	139

PINEAPPLE-BANANA SHAKE

1 cup fresh pineapple chunks
1 frozen banana, sliced
½ cup plain low-fat yogurt
½ cup skim milk
1 egg white
4 ice cubes, crushed
4 fresh pineapple wedges

Blend all ingredients except pineapple wedges until smooth and frothy. Pour into 4 frosted glasses and garnish each with pineapple wedge.

Serves 4

Per serving:	*Calcium* (mg)	*Fat* (g)	*Chol* (mg)	*Carbo* (g)	*Protein* (g)	*Calories*
	101	.7	2.5	20.1	3.9	96

PURPLE COW

1 cup buttermilk
½ cup grape juice
¼ teaspoon pure vanilla extract

Blend ingredients together for 30 seconds until frothy and pour into 2 frosted glasses.

Serves 2

Per serving:	*Calcium* (mg)	*Fat* (g)	*Chol* (mg)	*Carbo* (g)	*Protein* (g)	*Calories*
	198	1.1	4.5	15	4.4	88

TOFU TREAT

3 ounces soft tofu (bean curd)
1 medium frozen banana, sliced
1 cup skim milk
2 tablespoons wheat germ
4 ice cubes, crushed
Dash freshly grated nutmeg
Dash ground cinnamon

Blend all but last 2 ingredients together in a food processor or blender and serve with sprinkling of nutmeg and cinnamon.

Serves 2

Per serving:	*Calcium* (mg)	*Fat* (g)	*Chol* (mg)	*Carbo* (g)	*Protein* (g)	*Calories*
	143	1.9	1.5	14.7	6.2	95

TOMATO SHAKE

1 cup tomato juice or V-8
¾ cup plain low-fat yogurt
1 tablespoon fresh lemon juice
Dash celery salt
2 small stalks celery with leaves

Blend together all ingredients but celery stalks. Pour into 2 tall glasses and garnish with celery stalk.

Serves 2

Per serving:	*Calcium* (mg)	*Fat* (g)	*Chol* (mg)	*Carbo* (g)	*Protein* (g)	*Calories*
	172	1.4	5	12.5	5.8	82

HOT DRINKS

CINNAMON HOT CHOCOLATE

2 cups skim milk
2 tablespoons nonfat dry milk
1 tablespoon carob powder
½ teaspoon pure vanilla extract
2 cinnamon sticks

In a saucepan, combine the first 3 ingredients and bring to a simmer. Remove from heat and add vanilla, stirring in well. Pour into 2 cups and garnish each with a cinnamon stick.

Serves 2

Per serving:	*Calcium* (mg)	*Fat* (g)	*Chol* (mg)	*Carbo* (g)	*Protein* (g)	*Calories*
	367	.5	5	108	10	108

HOT RUSSIANS

1 tablespoon instant regular or decaf coffee
1 tablespoon frozen concentrated orange juice
3 tablespoons hot water
2 cups skim milk
2 tablespoons nonfat dry milk
½ teaspoon pure vanilla extract
1 teaspoon grated orange zest
½ teaspoon ground cinnamon

Combine instant coffee, orange juice concentrate, and hot water in a saucepan, mixing well. Add the skim milk and the nonfat dry milk and heat until simmering. Remove from heat and add vanilla. Pour into small cups and garnish each with grated orange zest and dash of cinnamon.

Serves 4

Per serving:	*Calcium* (mg)	*Fat* (g)	*Chol* (mg)	*Carbo* (g)	*Protein* (g)	*Calories*
	178	.2	2	8.7	5	57

12
BASICS

This chapter contains tips on ingredients and preparation techniques used throughout the book. It includes recipes for ingredients called for in the other recipes in this book. The inventive cook may enhance these basic recipes with personal variations. There is also a section on planning calcium-rich meals.

INGREDIENTS

Below is some helpful information on some of the ingredients used in the preceding recipes, as well as background on some calcium-rich substitutes.

Cheese

Cheese is a choice calcium food, a concentrated source of many of milk's nutrients. But attention must be paid to the cholesterol, fat, and sodium content of the many different varieties of cheese. There are choices to be made for taste and cooking method.

Cheese can be used in sandwiches, soups, salads, vegetables, sauces, casseroles, and dips; as a main dish; or with fruit for dessert. Cooking with cheese should be done quickly and at low temperatures, or by browning quickly under the broiler.

Read labels carefully for content when purchasing cheese, and store it, well wrapped, in the refrigerator. Some cheeses may be frozen. Imitation cheeses or cheese foods are made from vegetable oil and casein (milk protein), and, while they are low in cholesterol, their fat and calorie content remains high.

Low-fat cottage cheese (1%), part-skim ricotta cheese, and combinations with buttermilk, nonfat dry milk, yogurt, and skim milk play an important role in the high-calcium diet. Part-skim mozzarella cheese is also recommended for it melts well, imparts a nice flavor, and is lower in fat than many other cheeses. High-calcium, low-calorie recipes also call for small amounts of grated Parmesan or Romano and sapsago, a low-fat hard cheese with a sharp herbed flavor that is suitable for grating.

Cheddar cheese imparts a special flavor, but it is high in fat and calories, and a little can go a long distance.

The following chart will be helpful in making other cheese selections:

Cheese	*Calories*	*Fat (g)*	*Calcium (mg)*
LOW-FAT CHEESES			
Bon Bel, reduced-calorie, 1 oz. Mild, similar to Edam. Good for dessert or snacks.	60	4	209
Cheddar-style, 1 oz. Sharp flavor, good in sandwiches, casseroles, sauces. Some low-fat brands: Heidi Ann, Ryser, Tendale	70–83	4–5	200–260
Colby, Borden's Lite Line, 1 oz. Mild flavor for salads, sandwiches, snacks, casseroles.	50	2	200
Cottage Cheese, 4 oz. (½ cup):			
• Low-Fat 1%	80	1	69
• Low-Fat 2% Mild taste, good for baking, dips, blends, sauces.	101	2	77
Farmer Cheese, May-bud, 1 oz. Clean flavor, good for baking, molds, dumplings, cooking.	90	2	150
Mozzarella, part-skim, 1 oz. Mild flavor, good for pizzas, melts, sauces, grilled vegetables, and baked casseroles.	72	5	183
Muenster, Borden's Lite Line, 1 oz. Semisoft, for snacks, melts, sandwiches.	50	2	200

Cheese	*Calories*	*Fat (g)*	*Calcium (mg)*
Ricotta, part-skim, 1 oz. Semisweet flavor, good for cooked dishes, dips, combinations, fillings, desserts.	43	3	84
Swiss, 1 oz.:			
• Pasteurized Process Light 'n Lively, Kraft	71	4	214
• Borden's Lite Line Mild, nutty sweet flavor, used for salads, sandwiches, fondue, casseroles.	50	2	200
MODERATE-FAT CHEESES			
Edam, 1 oz. Mild, for appetizers, snacks, desserts with fruit.	101	8	207
Feta, 1 oz. White pickled cheese (sheep's milk), used in salads, soup, crumbled.	85	6	200
Goat's Milk Cheese, 1 oz. Good for dessert, salads, melts.	130	2	200
Parmesan, hard, 1 oz. Used grated in salads, breads, soups, sauces, vegetables, Italian dishes.	111	7	336
Romano, hard, 1 oz. Use grated as for Parmesan.	110	8	302
Swiss, 1 oz. Mild, nutlike taste, used for snacks, sandwiches, fondue, dessert with fruit.	107	8	272
PASTEURIZED PROCESS CHEESE PRODUCTS			
Laughing Cow Reduced Calorie Wedges, ¾ oz.	54	4.5	75
Kraft Light 'n Lively Singles, 1 oz.	77–84	6–7	143–161

Some cheese information used with permission of Dairy Nutrition Council Inc.

Formagg

A new product is currently hitting grocery markets nationwide. Formagg looks and tastes like real cheese, but it is made with polyunsaturated vegetable oil instead of butterfat, and casein, a high quality protein made from fresh milk. Formagg has 35 percent fewer calories than cheese, no cholesterol, and is loaded with vitamins and minerals. It is packaged shredded in plastic bags. Look for it in your grocer's cheese department, and use it as a replacement whenever natural cheese is required, in baking, as a topping, and for melt dishes. It contains 30 mg calcium, 0 mg cholesterol, and 75 calories per 1 ounce serving.

Ginger

Use fresh gingerroot whenever possible. Wash and grate without peeling. Store in bottle of sherry and refrigerate until ready to use.

Herbs

Herbs are the key to tastier dishes and sauces. Rosemary, tarragon, basil, oregano, dill, and many others can make the difference in fish dishes, dips, dressings, poultry recipes, and vegetables. If dried herbs are used rather than fresh, use about one-third of the fresh amount. To have a good year-round supply of basil on hand, gather the fresh basil leaves and place in blender or processor with a little water. Freeze in ice cube trays, then transfer to small storage containers and keep in freezer until ready to use.

Kefir

Kefir, which is now enjoying a renaissance on the American dairy scene, is delicious and may be used in place of plain yogurt, provided it is low-fat. Resembling sour cream in taste and texture, kefir may be acceptable for the lactose intolerant and provides about 85 calories and 160 mg of calcium per 8-ounce serving. Kefir cheese, another new product, contains 40 mg of calcium per 1-ounce serving.

Milk

The milk products called for in this cookbook are either nonfat, skim, or low-fat (1% fat, as in the case of cottage cheese).

- Buttermilk provides 99 calories per cup and 1% milkfat.
- Chocolate milk contains 179 calories per cup and 2% milkfat.
- 1% (low-fat) milk contains 102 calories per cup and 1% milkfat.
- 2% (low-fat) milk contains 121 calories and 2% milkfat per cup.
- Skim milk contains 86 calories and less than 1% milkfat per cup.
- Nonfat dry, instant, reconstituted milk contains 82 calories per cup and almost no fat.
- Evaporated skim milk contains 100 calories and about 300 mg of calcium per cup when diluted.
- Evaporated goat's milk contains 160 calories, 8 grams of fat, and 240 mg of calcium per 4-ounce serving, undiluted.
- Low-fat plain yogurt contains 144 calories and 4 grams of fat per cup.
- Nonfat yogurt contains 110 calories and 0 fat per cup.
- 1% (low-fat) cottage cheese contains 80 calories and 1 gram of fat per cup.

When shopping, purchase milk and milk products just before getting on the checkout line. Read the dates and refrigerate as soon as possible. Don't pour unused milk back into the container, but keep it refrigerated in a separate bowl. Keep dry milk tightly closed and store in a cool, dry place.

Goat's Milk and Cheese

Becoming increasingly important among the American cheeses, goat's milk cheese is an excellent calcium source and is lower in fat content than many other cheeses, with

40–50 percent of its calories coming from fat, compared to about 80 percent of calories coming from fat in regular cow's milk cheeses. Goat's milk and yogurt may also be tolerated better by those who cannot tolerate cow's milk.

Miracle Evaporated Goat Milk is enriched with folic acid and Vitamin D, and a 4-ounce serving contains 30 percent calcium. Powdered goat's milk is also available.

Miso

Miso has been used in Japanese cuisine for centuries and is a useful, calcium- and protein-laden paste made of fermented soybeans or barley. It can be purchased in health food stores and oriental markets. Use it in making dips and spreads, as a soup base, or in salad dressings. Miso is available in light and dark versions. It is low in fat and calories and considered by the Japanese to be a gift from the gods. Store in refrigerator.

Nonfat Dry Milk

An easy way to get a calcium boost is to add nonfat dry milk powder to recipes. It provides 50 milligrams of calcium per teaspoon. It can be added to chopped meats, soup, salad dressings, baked goods, drinks, and desserts. It disappears and is relatively tasteless. Buttermilk is also available in powdered form and is useful for baking and mixing blender beverages.

A Note on Lactose Intolerance

Lactose powder or Lactaid drops are available and can be added to milk to break down the lactose. Lactaid makes CalciMilk, which is available in many supermarket dairy departments. It has 500 mg of calcium per 8-ounce serving. The person who suffers lactose intolerance may be able to digest goat's milk, kefir, yogurt, and acidophilus milk. Soy milk also provides calcium and may be tolerated more readily. Soy milk may be found in natural food stores or made at home (see recipes at end of this chapter).

Nuts

Almonds and filberts, also known as *hazelnuts,* have a good amount of calcium. But they also contain high fat. Use them sparingly to add crunch. Buy them raw in a reliable health food store and beware of any soft or dried nuts as those may be toxic. Roast before using.

Seaweed

Minerals abound in the sea. Hence a number of different seaweeds are a valuable additional source of calcium. The Japanese rely on many different kinds of seaweed for their iron, magnesium, and calcium. Health food stores and Oriental markets are the best outlets. Here are some of the varieties to be found:

- *Hijiki*—Tastes a little like licorice. Very high in calcium. Use it in soup and salads.
- *Wakame*—A dark green leaf that needs to be soaked before using. Use in soups, on top of fish, in dressings.
- *Kombu*—A giant kelp plant that is found dried and shredded. Useful sprinkled over fish, chicken, rice, or vegetable dishes.
- *Nori*—Easy to toast as it comes in square sheets. Toast dried sheets of seaweed over stovetop burner or under broiler, then simply crumble over fish, salads, vegetables, pasta.
- *Dulse*—A red, Canadian seaweed used in cooking fish and stews.

None of these seaweeds have any calories to speak of, but they are chock-full of vitamins and minerals and also provide sodium.

Seaweed or kelp may be added to beans and legumes, soups, potatoes, rice, and other dishes.

Agar-agar also comes from the sea. It may be used in place of powdered gelatin. It is fairly costly and can be found in health food and Oriental stores. It delivers a mighty punch of calcium.

All of the seaweed products listed above may be ordered from Katagiri, 224 E. 59th St., New York, NY 10022. Eden Foods (Clinton, MI 49236) also imports and distributes many of these products. Maine Coast Sea Vegetables (Franklin, ME 04634; 207-565-2907) raises and packages a variety of American seaweeds.

Tofu

Tofu is available in health food stores, Oriental markets, and many supermarkets. Use the kind made with calcium sulfate. Tofu made with calcium sulfate yields 139 milligrams of calcium per 3.5-ounce serving. Keep covered with water in the refrigerator and change water daily. Use diced in soup, mashed in casseroles, or sliced and sautéed (see Tofu Sauté recipe at end of this chapter) or broiled after marinating. Tofu has no taste of its own and takes on the flavor of its companion ingredients. Because it soaks up water, it is best to drain the tofu between paper towels and under a weight to draw out the excess moisture. Tofu may be used in place of croutons over vegetables. Combined with frozen bananas or other fruit, it makes a fine dessert and can also be used to make spreads and appetizers, sauces, drinks, and dressings. Firm tofu cakes are better for cooking. The silken or soft tofu is best used for drinks or dessert mixtures.

Yogurt

Low-fat or nonfat plain yogurt is high in calcium. Yogurt is an acid food that helps to absorb iron and helps synthesize the B vitamins. It is more digestible than milk and is recommended for many people with lactose intolerance. It is an excellent source of protein and combines well with herbs, mustard, soy sauce, ginger, and sweeteners such as fructose, vanilla extract, fresh fruit, vegetables, and other skim milk products such as ricotta cheese, cottage cheese, and buttermilk. Draining yogurt (see Yogurt Sour Cream recipe at end of chapter) lets the whey escape and makes a solid, cheese yogurt that may be served plain or in recipes. Fresh batches of yogurt may be made as needed (see Your Own Yogurt recipe at end of chapter) by using a little yogurt mixed with milk.

SOME HOW-TO HINTS FOR PREPARATION

To Blanch

Vegetables retain their nutrients and crispness when cooked in boiling water for about 2 minutes and then refreshed quickly under cold water. They may then be served with dips or in salads with desired dressings. Nuts are also blanched in boiling water and the skins then rubbed away.

To Make Bread Crumbs

Place toasted or stale whole wheat bread in food processor and cut into chunks or finer, as desired. Store in tightly closed container in freezer until ready to use.

To Beat Egg Whites

Let egg whites stand at room temperature before beating. They will then whip more readily.

Freezing

Freeze summer berries and vegetables such as red or yellow bell peppers for use during the year. To freeze berries, do not wash, but pick them over and hull. Spread out on cookie sheet and place in freezer until solid. Transfer to baggies or freezer containers and store in freezer. Defrost before using. For the peppers, trim and slice into thin strips or dice them and freeze in the same manner.

To Make Ice Cream, Ices, and Sherbets

Ice cream machines are generally available, but if one is not on hand, there is an excellent method for making ices and sherbets. After mixing ingredients, pour into a shallow metal pan or metal ice tray. Cover and place in freezer until a band of ice appears around the edges. This may take 1–2 hours, depending on how efficient the freezer is. Break up the ice crystals by stirring briskly with a fork. Cover and return to freezer and repeat the beating and freezing procedure every 30 minutes or so. Just before serving, the mixture may be turned back into a food processor or turned into a bowl and beaten with an electric mixer. Serve when the mixture is slightly mushy after last beating or let it soften in refrigerator before dishing out.

To Julienne

To make thin julienne strips of bell peppers, citrus zest, carrots, celery, radishes, or other vegetables, trim away curved or spotted parts and cut into matchstick-shaped slices about 2 inches long, ¼-inch wide.

To Shuck Oysters

Always purchase fresh oysters from a reliable fish market. Scrub them thoroughly with a stiff brush under running water. Break off shells at the thin end. Hold an oyster in the palm of your hand with hinged end toward you. Force an oyster knife between shells at broken end and twist to force apart. Cut the large muscle, which is close to the flat upper shell. Break off and discard flat shell. Slide knife under the oyster meat to release it.

To Prepare Lobster

Cooking Lobster

To cook lobsters, fill a large kettle or steamer with water to depth of 1 inch and bring to boil. Place live lobsters in pot and cover. Steam for about 7 minutes, until lobster turns red, for lobsters weighing around a pound. For larger sizes, steam a bit longer. When cooked, lift lobsters out of pot and lightly push shells away from body to drain out excess fluid. Crack claws. Use a sharp knife to split lengthwise and remove the hard sand sac located between the eyes. All other parts of the lobster may be eaten.

To cut up a live lobster before cooking, drive the point of a sharp knife into the head on the underside of shell and force knife through to tail. This kills the lobster instantly and it may then be cut into smaller pieces.

To Prepare Nuts

Blanching Nuts

To blanch the nuts, drop them into a pot of boiling water for a few minutes. Remove, drain, and rub off the skins. They are now ready to be sliced or chopped.

Roasting Nuts

To roast nuts, spread them on a baking pan, sprinkle with a little cinnamon if desired, and bake in preheated 350°F oven for about 15 minutes, until lightly browned. Store in tightly closed container.

To Toast Seeds

To toast sesame, sunflower, or pumpkin seeds, heat a nonstick skillet, cover, and warm the seeds until they begin to pop. Shake the pan to keep them from burning. Remove and spread out on paper toweling to blot up any released oils. Store in a covered jar in refrigerator.

To Make Soup Stocks

Make large batches of your favorite recipe for vegetable, chicken, and beef broth and keep in the freezer in small, covered containers. When preparing a recipe that calls for stock, defrost ahead of time or heat in a saucepan. For small quantities, freeze the stock in ice cube trays and then store in baggies. When bones are used to make stock, be certain to add some plain vinegar, lemon juice, or tomatoes, as these acid ingredients draw out the calcium in the bones.

BASIC BEEF STOCK

4 pounds shin bones with meat
3 quarts water
1 cup sliced onions
1 cup sliced carrots
1 cup chopped celery
1 bay leaf
½ teaspoon dried thyme
8 whole peppercorns
4 sprigs fresh parsley
3 cloves
1 clove garlic

Cover shin bones with cold water in a large kettle and bring to a boil. Cook for two minutes and then drain. Return the bones to the kettle and add 3 quarts of water and the remaining ingredients. Return to boil and simmer for 4 hours, skimming off any fat and residue that accumulates. Strain stock and discard the solids. Refrigerate in a bowl and skim off any further fat. Then pour into individually measured containers and keep in freezer for future use.

Makes 10 cups

Per cup:	*Calcium* (mg)	*Fat* (g)	*Chol* (mg)	*Carbo* (g)	*Protein* (g)	*Calories*
	12	0	0	2.9	.4	13

CHICKEN STOCK

1 fryer chicken or stewing hen, skin removed
4 tablespoons vinegar
4 cloves garlic, chopped
2 ribs celery with tops, chopped roughly
2 medium onions, chopped
1 carrot, scraped and trimmed
1 parsnip, scraped and trimmed
6 sprigs parsley
1 bay leaf
6 peppercorns
8 cups water

Bring all ingredients to a boil in a large kettle. Cook uncovered over low heat for 15 minutes, removing any residue that accumulates. Reduce heat and simmer for 2 to 3 hours. Remove cover and let cool. Strain, pressing meat to draw out liquid. Save chicken pieces for use in enchiladas, salads, or other dishes. Discard other solids. Refrigerate in a bowl and skim off any further fat. Stock should be used within a few days or frozen in small containers for future use.

Makes 6 cups or 6 1-cup servings

Per serving:	*Calcium* (mg)	*Fat* (g)	*Chol* (mg)	*Carbo* (g)	*Protein* (g)	*Calories*
	39	1.3	22	11	9.6	94

VEGETABLE STOCK

Two methods are equally good for preparing a rich base for soup and sauce. The first is simply collecting the water left from cooking various vegetables. Blend together and store in refrigerator until ready to use. The second method is to use a kind of compost collection of all your vegetable parings and unused tops and excess vegetable pieces. Collect in a plastic bag. After a day or two add water or vegetable juices, place in saucepan, bring to a boil, and simmer for about 30 minutes. Then strain, place in small containers (or in an ice cube tray), and freeze until ready to use. (No nutrient figures are given since the amounts are negligible.)

BASIC RECIPES

BASIC BROWN RICE

1 cup brown rice, rinsed well until water runs clear
2 cups water or Vegetable Stock (see above)

Place rice in 2 cups of boiling liquid and cover. Simmer for 30 minutes over low heat without stirring, but checking to make certain there is enough liquid left. Remove from heat and let steam, covered, for another 10 minutes. Season, fluff and serve.

Vegetables such as peas, mushrooms, celery, onions, carrots, or scallions may be added, as well as any additional seasoning such as soy sauce or curry. These may be added before the steaming or stirred in later.

Note: The basic rule of thumb is two parts water to one part rice. To hasten cooking, soak rice for an hour or so before cooking. Rice may also be cooked in skim milk for added calcium. Cooked rice can be used to make pie crust. Spread 1 cup rice in pie tin, pat down, and bake in preheated 350°F oven for 10 minutes.

Makes 3 cups

Per ½-cup serving:	*Calcium* (mg)	*Fat* (g)	*Chol* (mg)	*Carbo* (g)	*Protein* (g)	*Calories*
	117	.3	1	1	2.4	117

BASIC WHITE SAUCE

1 tablespoon Best Butter (recipe follows)
1 tablespoon arrowroot
1 cup evaporated skim milk
⅛ teaspoon salt
⅛ teaspoon white pepper

Heat Best Butter in nonstick skillet, then stir in arrowroot. Gradually add milk, stirring until sauce thickens. Season with salt and pepper. For thicker sauce, add more butter and more arrowroot for each cup of milk.

Variations:

Cheese Sauce (Mornay): Add ¼ cup cubed cheddar, Parmesan, grated low-fat cheese or Formagg, and stir into the white sauce to melt.

Mushroom Cream Sauce: Add 6 chopped mushrooms and 1 chopped sautéed scallion to white sauce. Blend well and simmer for 5 minutes.

Makes 1 cup

Per 1-tablespoon serving of Basic White Sauce:	*Calcium* (mg)	*Fat* (g)	*Chol* (mg)	*Carbo* (g)	*Protein* (g)	*Calories*
	19	.8	1	1.8	1.1	23

Per 1-tablespoon serving of Cheese Sauce:	*Calcium* (mg)	*Fat* (g)	*Chol* (mg)	*Carbo* (g)	*Protein* (g)	*Calories*
	28	1.2	3	1.9	1.4	25

Per 1-tablespoon serving of Mushroom Cream Sauce:	*Calcium* (mg)	*Fat* (g)	*Chol* (mg)	*Carbo* (g)	*Protein* (g)	*Calories*
	29	.7	1	1.5	1.5	34

BEST BUTTER

1 cup polyunsaturated oil such as safflower, sunflower seed, corn, vegetable, soybean, walnut, vegetable, or combination
1 cup whipped butter
½ teaspoon salt

Mix ingredients together in blender or food processor. Store in refrigerator or freezer. May be herbed with garlic, scallions, mustard, tarragon, dill, etc. It is best when stored in the freezer.

Makes 2 cups

Per tablespoon:	*Calcium* (mg)	*Fat* (g)	*Chol* (mg)	*Carbo* (g)	*Protein* (g)	*Calories*
	1	11.1	11.6	0	.1	98

CREME FRAICHE

1 cup part-skim ricotta cheese
¼ cup buttermilk

Whip both ingredients in a blender until smooth. Heat in a small nonstick saucepan until just warm. Pour into a small jar and let stand for 8 hours at room temperature. Stir, cover, and chill until serving.

Makes 1 cup

Per serving:	*Calcium* (mg)	*Fat* (g)	*Chol* (mg)	*Carbo* (g)	*Protein* (g)	*Calories*
	46	1.3	5	1	1.9	23

GRAHAM CRACKER CRUST

2 tablespoons walnut oil
1 cup graham cracker crumbs (place crackers in food processor or blender to crumble)

Add walnut oil to the crumbs in blender or processor and blend well. Pat down in an 8-inch pie plate. Bake 10 minutes in preheated 350°F oven. Remove and let cool before filling. May be used with Carob Cream, Lime Filling, Peanut-Ricotta Sauce, or Mocha Filling (see index for pie recipes). Make your choice from the thick, creamy sauces or create your own. Also good lined with fruit and topped with yogurt, ricotta, or cottage cheese blends.

Makes one crust for a pie to serve 8

Per serving:	Calcium (mg)	Fat (g)	Chol (mg)	Carbo (g)	Protein (g)	Calories
	3	4.1	0	51	.6	57

GREAT GRAPE JELLY

1 cup unsweetened grape juice
3 tablespoons instant or granulated tapioca

Pour grape juice into saucepan and add tapioca. Let stand 10 minutes. Then bring to a boil over medium heat and stir. Remove from heat and let cool. Pour into a jar and keep refrigerated.

Makes 1 cup or 16 1-tablespoon servings

Per serving:	Calcium (mg)	Fat (g)	Chol (mg)	Carbo (g)	Protein (g)	Calories
	1	0	0	38	.1	16

LOW-FAT CREAM CHEESE

1 tablespoon nonfat dry milk
4 tablespoons Best Butter
2 tablespoons safflower oil
1 cup low-fat cottage cheese

Blend all ingredients together and refrigerate, covered.

Variation: Flavor with chives, scallions, or as desired.

Makes 1 cup or 16 1-tablespoon servings

Per serving:	Calcium (mg)	Fat (g)	Chol (mg)	Carbo (g)	Protein (g)	Calories
	12	3	4	.5	1.8	37

MAKE-BELIEVE MAYO

1 cup 1% (low-fat) cottage cheese
2 tablespoons safflower oil
1 tablespoon apple cider vinegar
½ teaspoon salt
Dash white pepper

Blend all ingredients until smooth. Refrigerate, covered, for at least 24 hours before using.

Variation: May be mixed with tomato paste, mustard, pickles, or any herbs as desired.

Makes 1 cup or 16 1-tablespoon servings

Per serving:	Calcium (mg)	Fat (g)	Chol (mg)	Carbo (g)	Protein (g)	Calories
	9	1.8	1	.4	1.8	25

PERFECT PIE CRUST

½ cup whole wheat flour
½ cup all-purpose unbleached flour
¼ teaspoon salt
3 tablespoons safflower oil
3 tablespoons ice water (or more if needed)
2 tablespoons buttermilk
1 egg white

Sift the flours and salt together into a mixing bowl, then stir in the oil, ice water, and buttermilk. Knead dough 3 or 4 times until it is moist and elastic. Roll into a ball, cover, and refrigerate 15 minutes. Place between 2 sheets of wax paper and roll dough into a 12-inch circle. Place in a 9-inch pie tin. Trim edges and finish by pressing with a fork or pastry knife. If baking the shell empty, prick a few holes in the dough. Brush shell with egg white and refrigerate for 10 minutes. Bake in preheated 350°F oven for 10 minutes, until brown. The same dough may be used to make tart shells, using a cup to cut the dough and baking the crust in muffin tins.

Makes 1 9-inch pie crust or 8 tart shells

Per serving:	*Calcium* (mg)	*Fat* (g)	*Chol* (mg)	*Carbo* (g)	*Protein* (g)	*Calories*
	12	7.1	0	14.7	3.1	133

SOY MILK

1 pound soy flour
3 quarts cold water
1 teaspoon pure vanilla extract
½ teaspoon salt
1 tablespoon crystalline fructose

Place flour and water in large saucepan and beat with a wire whisk until smooth. Cook over low heat, stirring, for about 20 minutes. Strain into a large bowl through cheesecloth-lined sieve. Mix in vanilla, salt, and fructose. Store, covered, in refrigerator.

Makes 3 quarts

Per 1-cup serving:	*Calcium* (mg)	*Fat* (g)	*Chol* (mg)	*Carbo* (g)	*Protein* (g)	*Calories*
	95	4.6	0	12.6	15.6	150

TOFU SAUTE

1 tablespoon low-sodium soy sauce
1 teaspoon walnut or safflower oil
1 drop sesame oil
1 cake firm tofu (bean curd) (about 1 cup), sliced into ½-inch pieces

Mix soy sauce and oils together. Press tofu slices between paper towels and place heavy weight on top for 15 minutes. When drained of excess moisture, place in marinade and turn to coat all pieces. Sauté in nonstick skillet until brown on both sides. Broil if preferred. This is a basic method for cooking tofu, which may then be used in salads, as garnish, in stir-fried vegetables, in casseroles, or just nibbled as is.

Serves 2

Per serving:	*Calcium* (mg)	*Fat* (g)	*Chol* (mg)	*Carbo* (g)	*Protein* (g)	*Calories*
	155	7.3	0	3.7	10.2	112

WHIPPED RICOTTA CREAM

¾ cup low-fat cottage cheese
⅓ cup part-skim ricotta cheese

Place cottage cheese in a small strainer and quickly rinse under cold water. Squeeze out any excess moisture. Place drained cottage cheese and ricotta in blender and whip until smooth. This is lovely as a topping combined with sugarless fruit conserve such as raspberry, apricot, or peach (use 2 teaspoons per cup of cheese).

Makes 1 cup or 16 1-tablespoon servings

Per serving:	*Calcium* (mg)	*Fat* (g)	*Chol* (mg)	*Carbo* (g)	*Protein* (g)	*Calories*
	19	.5	1.9	.5	1.8	14

YOGURT SOUR CREAM

Herbs (optional)
16 ounces plain low-fat or nonfat yogurt

If desired, mix herbs such as dill, tarragon, parsley, or caraway seed into the yogurt. Place yogurt in a cheesecloth-lined sieve and let it drip over a bowl in refrigerator for 4–6 hours or overnight, until the yogurt has the consistency of sour cream. The whey that drips out may be reserved for use in making soups or breads.

Variation: To make orange-flavored Yogurt Sour Cream, use 2 tablespoons concentrated frozen orange juice and a little cinnamon instead of the herbs for a sweet sauce.

Makes 1 cup or 16 1-tablespoon servings

Per serving:	*Calcium* (mg)	*Fat* (g)	*Chol* (mg)	*Carbo* (g)	*Protein* (g)	*Calories*
	26	.2	1	1	.7	9

Per serving of variation:	*Calcium* (mg)	*Fat* (g)	*Chol* (mg)	*Carbo* (g)	*Protein* (g)	*Calories*
	27	.2	1	1.8	.8	13

YOUR OWN YOGURT

1 quart skim milk or goat's milk
1 tablespoon plain low-fat yogurt

Pour milk into a saucepan and bring to a boil. Let cool to body temperature. Put the yogurt into a wide-mouthed jar and pour the milk over it, whisking. Cover and place in a warm spot for about 8 hours. Chill before using. Some of this yogurt may be used for future batches, but use the commercial yogurt as starter every so often.

Makes about 3 cups

Per cup:	Calcium (mg)	Fat (g)	Chol (mg)	Carbo (g)	Protein (g)	Calories
	411	.6	6	16.2	11.4	118

PLANNING CALCIUM-RICH MEALS

Plan meals so that there is a balance from the four essential food groups: milk, grains, fruit, and vegetables. Know the number of calories you need for each meal during the day, noting the total calories needed at different times of the day. The nutritional data that follow each recipe indicate the amount of calcium, protein, carbohydrate, fat, cholesterol, and calories it contains. Add up the numbers of all the dishes you select to get your total daily intake. After a while this will become second nature.

You may wish to make a meal of a soup, salad and bread. Or you may prefer an appetizer, entree, vegetable, and dessert. In planning nutritionally balanced meals, keep in mind the following recommended percentages of the food groups:

Protein	10–20 percent
Carbohydrates	50–60 percent
Fat	20–25 percent, with no more than 10 percent saturated
Cholesterol	no more than 200 milligrams daily or 100 milligrams cholesterol per 1000 calories
Fiber	25 grams per 1000 calories

Vary your food choices so that there are good balances of whole grains and seeds, fish, milk, and fresh vegetables.

Be aware of the following:

- Too much protein inhibits the effectiveness of calcium.
- Smoking and drinking alcohol may put you at greater risk of osteoporosis.

- Coffee is now known to prevent calcium absorption and its use should therefore be limited.
- Stress increases your need for calcium.
- Some medicines, such as cortisone, antacids, and laxatives may interfere with the absorption of calcium.
- Weight-bearing exercise on a regular basis helps to keep bones healthy.
- Young women should not exercise excessively, since this may cause amenorrhea which depletes calcium.
- Exposure to sunshine and vitamin D fortified milk products is essential to good bone growth.
- High fiber may interfere with calcium absorption.

Average calcium requirements:

- Children need 1,000 milligrams of calcium a day.
- Teenagers require 1,000 milligrams of calcium a day.
- Pregnant and nursing women require at least 1,500 milligrams a day.
- Pregnant and nursing teenagers need 1,600 or more milligrams daily.
- Adult women require 1,000 milligrams daily up to menopause and 1,500 milligrams thereafter, unless estrogen is prescribed.

APPENDIX 1
CALCIUM-RICH FOODS

DAIRY GROUP	Milligrams of Calcium
Milk, 1 cup	
Buttermilk	285
1% lowfat	300
2% lowfat	297
Skim	302
Evaporated skim milk, undiluted	738
Nonfat dry milk, unreconstituted	1508
Goat's milk, 1 cup	326
Yogurt, 1 cup	
Plain lowfat	415
Plain skim milk	452

MEAT GROUP	Milligrams of Calcium
Beans, dried, cooked, 1 cup	90
Oysters, raw, 7–9	113
Salmon, canned, with bones, 3 ounces	167
Sardines, canned, with bones, 3 ounces	372
Shrimp, canned, 3 ounces	99

FRUIT VEGETABLE GROUP	Milligrams of Calcium
½ cup, cooked, from fresh:	
Beet greens	72
Bok choy	126
Broccoli	68

FRUIT VEGETABLE GROUP	Milligrams of Calcium
Collards	179
Dandelion greens	147
Kale	103
Mustard greens	97
Spinach	84
Tofu, processed with calcium sulfate, 4 ounces	145
Turnip greens	267

GRAIN GROUP	Milligrams of Calcium
Soy flour, ½ cup	132
Waffle, 7-inch diameter	179
Pancakes, 4-inch diameter, serving of 2	116
Cornbread, 2 × 2 inches	94

NUTS (½ cup)	Milligrams of Calcium
Almonds	166
Brazil nuts	130
Hazelnuts	141
Pistachios	86
Sesame seeds	83
Pumpkin seeds	87

OTHER	Milligrams of Calcium
Blackstrap molasses, 1 tablespoon	137
Dried figs, 10	269
Miso, 1 tablespoon	150
Agar-Agar	400
Dulse (seaweed)	567
Hijiki (seaweed)	1400
Kombu (seaweed)	800
Wakame (seaweed)	1300

APPENDIX 2
MEASURES AND EQUIVALENTS

METRIC CONVERSION

Fluid Measurements

United States		Metric
4¼ cups or 1 quart plus 2 ounces	=	1 liter
2⅛ cups or 1 pint plus 1 ounce	=	½ liter
¼ teaspoon	=	1.25 milliliters
½ teaspoon	=	2.5 milliliters
1 teaspoon	=	5 milliliters
1 tablespoon	=	15 milliliters
¼ cup	=	63 milliliters
⅓ cup	=	84 milliliters
½ cup	=	125 milliliters
1 cup	=	¼ liter or 250 milliliters
1 pint	=	.473 liter
1 quart	=	.946 liter

Weight Measurements

United States		Metric
.035 ounce	=	1 gram
1 ounce	=	28.35 grams
3.5 ounces	=	100 grams
4 ounces	=	114 grams
8 ounces (1 cup)	=	226.78 grams
1 pound	=	454 grams
1 pound, 1.5 ounces	=	500 grams
2.21 pounds	=	1 kilogram

U.S. EQUIVALENT MEASUREMENTS

1 tablespoon	=	3 teaspoons
1/4 cup	=	4 tablespoons
1/3 cup	=	5 1/3 tablespoons
1/2 cup	=	8 tablespoons
3/4 cup	=	12 tablespoons
1 cup	=	16 tablespoons
1 pint	=	2 cups
1 quart	=	4 cups
1 gallon	=	4 quarts
1 pound	=	16 ounces

METRIC EQUIVALENT MEASUREMENTS

Fluid Measurements

1 deciliter	=	0.1 (1/10) liter
1 milliliter	=	0.001 (1/1000) liter

Weight Measurements

kilogram	=	1,000 grams (slightly more than 2 pounds or about 2.2 pounds)
gram	=	0.001 (1/1000) kilogram
milligram	=	0.001 (1/1000) gram

OVEN TEMPERATURES

200°F—very low
300°F—low
325°F—moderately low
350°F—moderate
375°F—moderately hot
400°F—hot
450°F—very hot
550°F—broil

INDEX